TUNISIA

ANN JOUSIFFE

NEW
HOLLAND

NEW
HOLLAND

★★★ Highly recommended
★★ Recommended
★ See if you can

Fifth edition published in 2010
by New Holland Publishers (UK) Ltd
London • Cape Town • Sydney • Auckland
10 9 8 7 6 5 4 3 2 1

Garfield House, 86-88 Edgware Road
London W2 2EA
United Kingdom

80 McKenzie Street
Cape Town 8001
South Africa

Unit 1, 66 Gibbes Street
Chatswood, NSW 2067
Australia

218 Lake Road
Northcote, Auckland
New Zealand

Distributed in the USA by
The Globe Pequot Press
Connecticut

Keep us Current
Information in travel guides is apt to change, which is
why we regularly update our guides. We'd be grateful
to receive feedback if you've noted something we
should include in our updates. If you have new
information, please share it with us by writing to the
Publishing Manager, Globetrotter, at the office nearest
to you (addresses on this page). The most significant
contribution to each new edition will receive a free
copy of the updated guide.

Publishing Manager: Thea Grobbelaar
DTP Cartographic Manager: Genené Hart
Editors: Thea Grobbelaar, Deidré Petersen, Tarryn Berry,
Sean Fraser, Peter Duncan, Mary Duncan
Cartographers: Reneé Spocter, Carryck Wise, Elaine Fick,
Carl Germishuys
Design and DTP: Nicole Bannister, Lellyn Creamer,
Éloïse Moss
Picture Researchers: Shavonne Govender, Colleen
Abrahams, Rowena Curtis
Updated by: Robin Gauldie

Reproduction by Hirt & Carter (Pty) Ltd, Cape Town
Printed and bound by Times Offset (M) Sdn. Bhd.,
Malaysia.

This guidebook has been written by independent
authors and updaters. The information therein represents
their impartial opinion, and neither they nor the publishers accept payment in return for including in the
book or writing more favourable reviews of any of the
establishments. Whilst every effort has been made to
ensure that this guidebook is as accurate and up to date
as possible, please be aware that the facts quoted are
subject to change, particularly the price of food, transport and accommodation. The Publisher accepts no
responsibility or liability for any loss, injury or inconve-
nience incurred by readers or travellers using this guide.

CONTENTS

1
Introducing Tunisia

Among the giants of North African countries, Tunisia sits like a small triangle resting against the **Mediterranean Sea**, its southerly point piercing down into the **Sahara Desert**. It is a land with an ancient and mixed heritage with its own distinctive culture and traditions. The most open and accessible of all the Maghreb countries, Tunisia offers visitors the best of both worlds: miles of pure sand beaches with a Mediterranean lifestyle, combined with the traditional North African culture of both the Sahara Desert and the mountain villages of the north.

The dominant culture of Tunisia is **Arab**, although many other peoples have contributed to the heritage of the country. The Phoenicians, Romans, Turks and French have all left their imprint. The result is that the country is rich in things to see and experience – from magnificent mosques and souks to the classical ruins of antiquity.

Since independence in 1956, Tunisia has undergone considerable modernization and development and now has a relatively sophisticated infrastructure. The capital, **Tunis**, is a bustling city in the north of the country with a fascinating old medina surrounded by colonial architecture and contemporary buildings, plus all the comforts of a modern city.

With its hot Mediterranean summers and mild winters, Tunisia can be enjoyed all the year round, and its proximity to Europe makes it a very popular winter destination for holidaymakers.

TOP ATTRACTIONS

*** Tunis medina: the heart of the capital city.
*** Dougga: most impressive of the Roman ruins in Tunisia.
*** Tabarka: a beautiful, unspoiled beach resort.
** Kairouan's Great Mosque: monumental architecture.
*** The Sahara: take a trip to the world's greatest desert.
*** The Bardo Museum: magnificent mosaics.
** Carthage: worth visiting for the history alone.
** El Jem: a spectacular Roman amphitheatre.
** Bulla Regia: see the unique underground villas.

Opposite: *The Tunisian tradition of horsemanship is displayed at festivals.*

TUNISIA FACT FILE

Tunisia lies on the coast of North Africa bordered by Algeria on the west and Libya on the east. To the north and east is the Mediterranean Sea.

The population of Tunisia is about 10 million: ¾ live in the coastal region, and 1½ million in the capital, Tunis.

With an area of 164,000km² (63,304 sq miles), Tunisia is by far the smallest of the North African countries. It has a coastline of 1148km (713 miles). Yet it has four different topographic regions: the mountains of the north, a low-lying plateau in the centre, known as the chotts, and the Sahara in the south.

The highest point is Jebel Chambi (1544m/5143ft) just west of Kasserine.

Below: *The endless expanse of the Sahara is a great attraction for visitors.*

THE LAND
Mountain, Coast and Desert

Tunisia has a great variety of landscapes that stretch from rugged **coastline** in the north of the country through **salt-lake flats** in the middle to rolling **dunes** in the south. The sandstone hills in the north are the westerly extension of the **Atlas** mountain range which ends in the Cap Bon peninsula. These northerly hills have a cooler climate than the rest of the country and are covered in pine forests and vineyards.

The coast of Tunisia is a long, sandy beach punctuated with rocky outcrops and interrupted by the three major bays: the **Gulf of Tunis**, the **Gulf of Hammamet** and the **Gulf of Gabès**. There are also a few offshore islands and some, like the **Kerkennah Islands** and **Djerba** in the south, are inhabited.

The middle third of the country is flat and much of it lies at sea level, with a series of salt lakes – known as **chotts**, and only a few feet deep – covering large areas of the land. These areas are surrounded by the arid Sahara Desert which stretches down to the southern borders of Tunisia and beyond. **Oases** punctuate the wilderness with picturesque palm groves fed by freshwater pools.

Seas and Shores

The coast of Tunisia is on the Mediterranean Sea and enjoys a mild climate all year. The shore is mostly sandy and the land shelves gradually into the shallow seas – water temperature is therefore quite high for most of the year – but there are rocky headlands, notably the **Cap Bon** peninsula and those around **Tabarka** in the north. The coastal strip has the highest population density and is popular in summer with both Tunisians and foreign visitors.

Above: *The deep blue Mediterranean coast of Tunisia has wonderful sandy beaches.*

Some offshore oil fields to the south of the country, such as the **Bouri Oil Field**, are being exploited, while others await exploration.

The Chotts

These vast, shallow, salt lakes cover immense areas in the central part of Tunisia and the largest, **Chott El Jerid**, has a causeway running right across it to accommodate traffic. In winter, when the water is high, the chotts are swampy areas of unstable ground, but in summer the surfaces harden and crystallize into a gleaming white surface which may sometimes be used for sand yachting. These expanses are as flat as a bowl of milk and often produce mirages in the shimmering heat.

Climate

The climate varies from north to south. The **northern** part of the country enjoys a **Mediterranean** climate while the **Saharan** heat in the **south** can be intense and dry. On the coast, sea breezes may take the edge off the midsummer heat and make life bearable, but temperatures in July and August can still reach over 30°C. In the desert interior, temperatures can soar to a scorching 40°C or more in the midsummer months.

CONSERVATION

In recent years, Tunisia has made considerable effort to conserve its ecological heritage and has turned eight natural areas into **national parks**:
- Islands of **Zembretta** and **Zembra** in the Gulf of Tunis;
- **Ichkeul**, near Bizerte (mountain, lake and marshland);
- **Chaambi**, near Kasserine (pine forest and the highest peak in Tunisia);
- **Bou Hedma**, near Gafsa (the last pre-Saharan savanna);
- **Bou Kornine**, south of Tunis (forest vegetation and varied fauna);
- **Feija**, near Ghardimaou in the north (cork and oak forest with rare orchids);
- **Sidi Toui**, on the edge of the Sahara.

Above: *Before desert tourism arrived it was the humble date palm which provided many Tunisians with a living – harvesting and selling the succulent Deglet Nour dates which are famous worldwide.*

In the winter months, the coast is still warm but subject to occasional rain and storms, and although the temperatures in the desert interior are high during the day, they drop rapidly – sometimes to below freezing point – at night.

Flora and Fauna

One image that sums up North Africa is that of the palm tree. In the desert oases, the palm is often the only productive crop and whole communities have, in the old days, made a living from growing and harvesting dates.

The **date palm** grows to a height of 18m (60ft) with a straight, rough-textured trunk topped with a cluster of barbed leaves. Female trees also have a number of branching spikes that bear 200 to 1000 dates each. A date cluster may weigh up to 12kg (26lb) and each year a single tree can produce 270kg (600lb) of dates. Trees begin to bear fruit at the age of eight. They reach maturity at 30 and begin to decline at 100 years. Dates contain 40% water, 58% sugar and 2% each of fat, protein and minerals.

Other trees and shrubs include **acacia**, **oleander**, **tamarisk** and **eucalyptus**. In spring the coastal and higher areas are covered with flowers, including **wild orchids**, **narcissi** and **crocus**. The ubiquitous **prickly pear** was originally introduced to form defensive hedges and now grows rampant.

Tunisia's two main cultivated crops are **olives** and **dates**, closely followed by a variety of **citrus fruit**, **figs**, **grapes** and **wheat**, which is grown in the Sahel. Aleppo pine forests and cork trees also grow in the northern part of the

COMPARATIVE CLIMATE CHART	TUNIS				GABÈS				GAFSA			
	WIN	SPR	SUM	AUT	WIN	SPR	SUM	AUT	WIN	SPR	SUM	AUT
	JAN	APR	JULY	OCT	JAN	APR	JULY	OCT	JAN	APR	JULY	OCT
AVERAGE TEMP. °C	14	21	32	25	16	23	32	27	13	25	38	25
AVERAGE TEMP. °F	58	70	90	77	61	74	89	81	58	77	101	81
RAINFALL mm	64	36	3	51	23	10	0	31	18	15	3	13
RAINFALL in	2.5	1.5	0	2	1	0.5	0	1	0.5	0.5	0	0.5

country providing **timber** and **cork** (which is useful for stoppering the local bottles of wine).

The list of **wildlife** hunted to non-existence in Tunisia makes depressing reading. Gazelles, lions, panthers, oryx, moufflon, baboons and hyenas are all long gone; victims of the French rule which saw much over-hunting. There are, however, still some **wild mammals** left in the country, such as the **fennec, wild boar, porcupine** and **fox**. Some wildlife reserves have been established and you can again see **ostrich**, once a common bird in North Africa. **Domestic animals** are the most numerous mammals, and include **dromedary camels, sheep, goats** and **donkeys**. **Cows** are also raised in the north of the country for both meat and milk.

Lizards and **snakes** are common and there are some poisonous species such as the **horned viper**. However, because they are rather shy creatures, you are unlikely to be bitten.

Tunisia is home to many varieties of **migrating birds**, and one of the great sights is that of hundreds of pink **flamingos** wading in the shallow chotts during the spring. Keen bird-watchers will also spot **spoonbills, avocets, sandpipers, dunlin, redshank** and **stints**. Further inland you can see (and hear) **larks, wheatears, trumpeter finches** and **hoopoe larks**. The best time for bird-watching is early morning or evening.

FENNECS

This is the name of the pale-coloured **desert fox** native to North Africa and Arabia. It is small in size and able to live for long periods without water, getting all its nourishment from the small rodents, lizards and birds on which it feeds.

The most striking thing about the fennec is the enormous size of its ears, which help regulate its body temperature and give it an appealing look. It is unusual to see one during the day as it sleeps in its burrow in the sand, coming out to hunt at night when it is cooler.

Below: *Gazelles were common in the Sahara until the late 20th century; captive breeding programs are now trying to increase the gazelle population with a view to releasing them into the wild.*

IN THE BEGINNING...

It is thought that human beings first settled in North Africa around one million years ago. The earliest traces of habitation date from the early **Paleolithic Age**, 500,000 years ago. At this time, the Sahara was fertile and the green savannah supported a large variety of game. There followed several climate swings from wet to dry and back again.

The late Paleolithic Age dating from 40,000 years ago saw a culture called the **Aterians**, who left traces on the Cap Bon peninsula. Between 13,000 and 5000BC, there were two main cultural groups: the **Ibero-Mauretanian** culture in the northern coastal region and the better-known **Capsian Man**, whose artefacts were found around Gafsa.

From 5000BC onwards, the more advanced **Neolithic** culture came to North Africa and there is evidence of contact with peoples across the Mediterranean.

HISTORY IN BRIEF

The land that is now Tunisia has been settled for at least 6000 years by **Berber** tribes. Indications of earlier human habitation nevertheless go back a lot further, and the earliest human artefacts are 200,000 years old. **Neanderthal man** also left traces of his stone tools dating from around 70,000 years ago up to 40,000 years ago.

The Berber tribes lived for 3000 years in their semi-nomadic, hunter-gatherer existence until the coming of the next wave of settlers, who heralded Tunisia's entry into history.

The Phoenicians

By 1000BC, the Phoenician traders from the eastern Mediterranean had established themselves as the most accomplished mariners in the Mediterranean. Their ships plied their trade from the Atlantic to the Levant and along the coastline they established safe anchorages wherever they could find them. These safe harbours started as stopovers for Phoenician traders but soon grew into permanent settlements and eventually formed larger towns and cities, the most important of which became **Carthage**.

Over time, the Phoenicians intermarried with the local Berbers and spread their culture, language and alphabet – and many other advanced skills – among the population. Their growth continued until 550BC when the **Greeks** began to challenge the Phoenicians for supremacy of the sea. The Phoenicians lost their homeland in Lebanon to the **Babylonians** and, to protect their interests, formed a league of city states under the leadership of Carthage.

From this point, the **Carthaginians** became the dominant force in the western Mediterranean, but their dominance was not to last long. In 480BC, the Greeks mounted a campaign and drove the Carthaginians south to the interior where they concentrated on developing trade routes into Africa. In 410BC, the Carthaginians returned and gathered an army against the Greeks, but, despite inflicting damage on the Greeks in Sicily, their

Left: *This rare Punic tomb survives in the Museum at Carthage.*

victory was short-lived. Berber revolts and a continual round of battle with the Greeks in Sicily took their toll.

Meanwhile, the **Romans** were rapidly becoming a force to be reckoned with and Rome's ambitions for an empire brought them into conflict with their former allies in Carthage. A dispute arose over Sicily and what was to become known as the **first Punic war** broke out in 264BC, ending in 241BC with the Romans seizing the initiative and launching an attack on Tunisian soil. They landed at Cap Bon and started yet another Berber revolt followed by a siege on Carthage. The decisive moment of the Carthaginians' downfall came in a naval battle in 242BC in which they surrendered to the Romans.

Two more Punic wars followed in 218–201BC, in which **Hannibal** launched his famous attack over the Alps on elephants, and again in 149–146BC, which ended with the complete destruction of Carthage: her people killed or sold into slavery and the great city levelled to the ground. The general, **Scipio**, had the land ploughed with salt to make it barren and cursed the site to prevent the city ever rising again.

The Romans

Following the fall of Carthage, Tunisia became a Roman province and, only 24 years after the destruction of the city, a new city was proposed by **Caius Gracchus**. The 'curse for

PHOENICIAN SAILORS

The world's first great age of exploration came from the Phoenicians during the first millennium BC, and their extraordinary skills as navigators soon made them masters of the Mediterranean. Their colonies started out as safe harbours where traders would anchor for a night or two, and these valuable harbours were kept strictly secret in the beginning – but soon grew into permanent settlements. **Carthage** was one such settlement which grew so large that it became independent of its mother state, **Phoenicia** (what is modern-day Lebanon).

It is thought that Phoenician sailors were the first to navigate by the **Pole Star** and, with this knowledge, they travelled far beyond the Mediterranean. Evidence shows Phoenician influences in India and Sri Lanka as well as Cornwall, the Canaries and the Azores. It is even thought that they circumnavigated Africa in a mission that took three years.

Above: *The magnificent Roman amphitheatre at El Jem is where huge numbers of valuable wild animals would regularly be set loose in the arena to fight each other, or gladiators, to the death, attracting tens of thousands of spectators.*

all time' seemed very short-lived indeed. However, it was only when former Carthaginian territories had been annexed and **Utica** became the new capital of the province that Carthage was finally rebuilt as a Roman city.

The Roman colony of **Africa Nova** was generally peaceful and, once the local Berber kings had been quelled and the land unified, it was placed under senate control and fully incorporated into the Roman Empire. Along with other parts of North Africa such as Libya and Egypt, Rome came to depend upon the grain produced here to feed the Empire. Other produce such as wine and olive oil also made Africa Nova wealthy and important.

During the first century AD, the Romans built a number of impressive cities in what is now Tunisia: Dougga, Bulla Regia, Thuburbo Majus, Sbeitla and, of course, Julia Karthago, on the site of Carthage. Smaller towns also sprung up in their hundreds and paved roads were introduced, many of which follow the routes of today's highways. The

HISTORICAL CALENDAR

814BC Carthage founded by Phoenician settlers.
146BC Romans destroy Carthage and set up the province of Africa Proconsularis.
312AD Emperor Constantine converts to Christianity.
439AD Vandals capture Carthage.
533AD General Belisarius defeats the Vandals for Emperor Justinian.
670AD First wave of Arab invasions and the foundation of Kairouan.

698AD Arab conquest completed, ushering in new golden age under the Aghlabids.
739AD Revolt of the Berber tribes against Arab rulers.
915AD The Fatimids succeed and found Mahdia as their capital.
1520–80 The Hapsburg-Ottoman war leaves Tunisia in the hands of the Ottomans.
1705 The Husseinite dynasty established.
1881 Following financial crisis, French occupy Tunisia.

1934 The foundation of the pro-independence Neo-Destour Party.
1956 Tunisia becomes independent.
1957 Founding of the Republic by President Habib Bourguiba.
1987 Bourguiba deposed by President Ben Ali.
1994 Ben Ali re-elected as president with 99% of vote.
2000 Bourguiba dies, still under house arrest, aged 97.
2004 and **2009** Ben Ali re-elected as president.

standard of living was undoubtedly high and the Bardo Museum's superb collection of mosaics from this period – during which time the art of the mosaic reached its apex in North Africa – derived from the villas of these wealthy merchants. This was Roman Africa in its heyday, ruled by the Severan dynasty whose founder, **Septimius Severus**, was himself of African origin, being a native of Leptis Magna (in modern-day Libya).

As part of the Roman world, Tunisia also received **Christianity** into its midst. There were many converts in North Africa, though at first these African Christians were persecuted without mercy. **St Perpetua** and **St Felicity** were just two martyrs who lost their lives in the amphitheatres, torn to pieces by wild animals. Eventually, Christianity brought great pressure to bear on the Roman rulers of North Africa. The new faith gained in strength until the 3rd century AD when the weakness of Rome, combined with increasing strength of the Berber tribes, broke the hold of Rome in the province once and for all. Christianity became openly practised, although it did not become legal until the reign of **Constantine** in 333AD.

The Vandals

Rome was coming under increased attacks by hostile tribes from the north. Repeated offensives by one tribe, the Vandals, eventually caused Rome to buckle and, in 429AD, an army of 80,000 Vandals swept down through Europe and crossed into North Africa across the straits of Gibraltar. By 431, the province – apart from Carthage, which held out for eight more years – had fallen under their rule. **Genseric**, the Vandal leader, proclaimed himself king and dismantled the existing power structure using Carthage as a base for carrying out raids across the Mediterranean, including the sack of Rome itself. The Vandal rule continued until 533, when the province was targeted by the Byzantine general **Belisarius** who placed a high priority on the recapture of Rome's Western Empire.

BELISARIUS (C 505–565)

A Byzantine general, Belisarius was one of history's 'great military geniuses'. He was given command by Emperor Justinian I and distinguished himself in action against the **Persians**, where he defeated an army vastly outnumbering his own. He was sent to North Africa in 533 to fight the **Vandals**, who had ruled in a reign of terror for a century. He was victorious within one year and took their king back to Constantinople as prisoner. He later chalked up further victories in **Sicily** and on mainland **Italy**.

His fall from favour came as a result of court intrigues but he was recalled 10 years later to repel a **Bulgarian** invasion which threatened Constantinople. Despite a spell in prison over an accusation of conspiracy in 562, he managed to live out his old age peacefully.

Below: *The Romans left a legacy of fine mosaics, like this detail depicting the seasons surrounded by scenes of animals.*

Opposite: *The elaborate
decoration inside the
dome of the Barber's
Mosque in Kairouan dis-
plays all the ornate tastes
of the Ottoman era.*
Right: *The sophisticated
Aghlabids in the 9th
century were talented
engineers and built these
circular reservoirs near
Kairouan, of which two
still work following
restoration in 1969.*

Byzantine Rule

With the rise of the Eastern Roman Empire, then based
at Byzantium, the days of the barbarian rulers were
numbered. The renowned general, Belisarius, sailed to
Sicily and recaptured the island from the **Ostragoths**
before taking Africa. It took only two decisive battles to
oust the Vandals from their position of power, though
the Berber tribes of the interior were a different matter.
After prolonged resistance the Berber tribes were finally
subdued.

   There followed a period of prosperity and expansion,
when many **churches** were built in Carthage and the port
area was restored for trade. For 150 years, Tunisia was thus
ruled by the Byzantine Empire, albeit from afar.

   In 646 the **Prefect Gregory** declared the province
independent of Byzantium, but only a year later the entire
North Africa fell to the Arabs in a wave of conquest which
would change North Africa forever.

The Arabs

After the Prophet **Mohammed** died in Medina in 632AD, the
new religion of Islam spread throughout the Arabian
Peninsula and, during the following decade, his heirs set
about conquering the known world. They started with
Syria, Egypt and Persia and soon turned their attentions to
Africa. In 647 an army invaded Tunisia and defeated
Gregory's forces at **Sbeitla** but it wasn't until 694 to 698
that the Arabs finally took control, set up their capital at
Kairouan and appointed an Emir.

Despite Berber mutinies against their new masters, the Arabs entered a golden age under the **Aghlabids**. They developed agriculture and introduced new crops from the East, in addition to which the trans-Saharan trade route brought gold and slaves to add to their wealth. Their cultural legacy was long-lasting and, by the time their era came to an end, most of the inhabitants spoke Arabic rather than Berber.

The Muslim world was at that time riven with dissenting groups. One such was the extreme **Shia Ismaili** group who believed in the right of the descendants of Ali (the husband of the Prophet's daughter, **Fatima**) to be Caliph (supreme ruler of the Islamic world). The Fatimids, as they came to be

known, began their bid for power by conquering Tunisia and establishing their leader in a citadel at **Mahdia**. Eventually they conquered Egypt and moved the capital to Cairo in 973, leaving Tunisia in the hands of their allies the **Zirids**.

Rebellions from local tribes and the constant in-fighting between rival Arab tribes continued on and off for the next 400 years. Nevertheless, during the latter part of the **Hafsid dynasty** Tunisia regained extensive trading contact with Europe. The trading state that emerged at this time, with its capital at **Tunis**, closely resembled Tunisia of today.

However, this period of relative stability came to an end when Tunisia became embroiled in the struggle between Christian Spain (who had recently ousted the Moors) and the Turks who had just taken Constantinople. Fighting was fierce but eventually the **Ottoman Turkish forces** won and North Africa entered a long period of Ottoman rule.

ARABIC SCRIPT

Arabic script is a highly decorative form of writing which reads from right to left. Calligraphers have perfected the art of incorporating the script into many decorative forms. The most used are **Diwali** script which is flowing and complex and **Kufic** script which is geometric and angular. From the early days of Islam, Arabic writing and geometry replaced figurative art which was forbidden, as portraying living things was not permitted. These forms of Arabic writing can be seen on buildings, pottery and as artworks in their own right, giving Arabic works of art their own distinctive style.

Turkish Rule

The Ottoman Empire significantly changed the face of North Africa and the Middle East, and was to last from 1574 until 1704. The Ottomans brought a new administration, culture and architecture to the region. They were Muslim but not Arab and Tunisia became a regency of the **Sultan** who appointed a complex system of **Pashas**, who shared their power with the **Deys** (military commanders) and **Beys** (civil administrators). Soon a hereditary line of Beys, known as the **Muradids**, took hold of the country.

By the mid-17th century, **European** traders were allowed back in. The French were the first to build a consulate in 1659 in the Tunis medina, but the economy was still firmly in the grip of the corsair pirates who preyed heavily upon Mediterranean shipping.

Soon the Muradids were ousted by the **Husaynid dynasty** of Beys who continued until 1881, during which time they secured a large degree of autonomy for Tunisia and ties with the Sultan were loosened. The country prospered from the proceeds of piracy until the early 19th century, when the **US navy** launched attacks on Tunis and other Barbary cities, bringing to an end lucrative trade.

As a result, Tunisia was plunged into financial crisis and debts piled up. The chief creditors were France, Italy and Great Britain who were, at the time, hatching imperialist plots against North Africa. In 1830 France conquered neighbouring Algeria and by 1881 negotiated a treaty with the Bey of Tunis making Tunisia a **French** protectorate.

PIRATES

The **Corsairs** of the Barbary coast were notorious from the 16th to 19th centuries as the scourge of the Mediterranean and beyond. Piracy arose after the triumph of the **Christians** over the **Muslim Moors** in Spain, who fled to North Africa, and the consequent establishment of virtually independent city states which paid little heed to the Sultan. They attacked ships and took prisoners into slavery as well as for booty. The raids began as retaliation against Spain but became a thriving enterprise. Europe and the USA tried to quash the pirates, but it was only after the French occupied Algiers in 1830 that the pirates were suppressed.

The French Protectorate

Under the French protectorate, the Bey was still nominally the ruler – but with a French general in residence pulling the strings. French immigration followed and large colonial estates replaced the former Tunisian smallholdings, with local farmers becoming landless labourers. In addition to French colonists, there were huge numbers of Italian settlers fleeing poverty in southern Italy.

The situation was a recipe for revolt, but the French managed to suppress patriotic movements as they appeared – including the Young Tunisians' independence movement – and held control for several more decades. In the 1920s, however, various nationalist movements united to form the **Destour Party**, which – despite being disbanded – re-emerged in the economic depression of the 1930s. The party was organized by **Habib Bourguiba** and had links with leftwing and nationalist groups in France, Morocco and Algeria. The nationalist momentum was temporarily halted by **World War II** when Tunisia became important in Axis military operations and, along with the rest of North Africa, became a theatre of war. After the surrender of the Axis powers, Tunisia was returned to the Free French government who arrested alleged fascist sympathizers and deposed the Bey. Not at all popular with the Tunisian people, this re-ignited the nationalist movement.

BIRTH OF A NATION

Tunisia's movement to rid itself of colonial rule began in the late 19th century when the power vacuum left by the fading **Ottoman Empire** began to inspire people to thoughts of independence and democracy. By the 1880s, Tunisia was caught in a grab for territory between Britain, France and Italy in which the **French** won Tunisia. The figurehead Beys were under the control of the French and Tunisians began to demand more power in government. Despite backing France in World War II, the move away from colonialism was inevitable.

Political agitation followed and demands for power sharing gradually developed into a movement for independence. The French reluctantly gave up power in Tunisia but were in a weak position following World War II and, in 1956, they at last granted full **independence** to Tunisia and a republic was declared.

Opposite: *During the Second World War heavy fighting took place in North Africa, including a series of running battles in Tunisia from November 1942 to May 1943.*
Left: *The flag of Tunisia was first adopted in 1831, and its traditional Islamic symbols have changed little since then.*

TILEWORK

All throughout North Africa tilework has become a major feature of both religious and secular buildings. The intricate geometric designs come originally from Moorish Andalucía where they developed over the centuries. After the fall of Spain to the Christians, many Andalucíans fled to parts of North Africa taking their skills with them. Vibrant blues and greens used in the tiles make them attractive souvenirs and you can buy single tiles or whole decorative panels to reassemble at home.

In 1945 Habib Bourguiba was forced to take refuge in Cairo to avoid arrest as an agitator, but the following year France granted Tunisia a semi-autonomous status. In 1949, Bourguiba returned and continued to push for full independence. Time was clearly running out for the colonialists and, under increasing pressure from riots and civil disturbance, Tunisia finally gained full **independence** in 1956, as a constitutional **monarchy** under the Bey of Tunis to begin with.

Independence

Habib Bourguiba formed the first assembly and held elections. The Bey was removed and a **Republican** constitution was thus adopted. Bourguiba became the first president of Tunisia and became known as the 'father of the nation'. Fearing anti-French reprisals, many of the former colonists subsequently fled the country, taking both their skills and their capital with them. Tensions between France and Tunisia began to escalate and, despite a brief hiatus in 1960, eventually erupted into fierce fighting when France refused to withdraw her navy from the base at **Bizerte**. The siege finally ended with 1300 Tunisian casualties, and both sides accepted the UN ruling for a cease-fire. In 1963, France reluctantly left Bizerte.

During the 1960s Tunisia aligned itself closer to the **Arab** world, and a whole new set of problems emerged from

Left: *In the 1970s Bourguiba worked to develop the country's economy; today Tunisia is one the world's major producers of phosphates.*
Opposite: *Since the advent of package tours in the 1960s, Tunisia has received many visitors.*

this relationship. When Bourguiba proposed a peace settlement between **Israel** and the Arab states in 1965, it was rejected by both sides and this then served to strain Tunisia's relations with the Arabs, especially Saudi Arabia and Egypt.

During the 1970s, Habib Bourguiba concentrated on developing the country's economy but, having given refuge to **Yasser Arafat** and several hundred PLO followers expelled from Lebanon in 1982, the Israelis later led an air attack in 1987.

The same year, the ageing and increasingly rather senile Bourguiba was forced to step down and was replaced by the then Prime Minister, **Zine al-Abidine Ben Ali**. The new president brought in several reforms, freeing political prisoners, legalizing opposition parties and also lifting restrictions on the press. In the following free elections, Ben Ali's party won all the seats in parliament.

During the 1990s, however, Ben Ali found himself having to deal with a rising **Islamic fundamentalist** element who dislike his continued support of the Algerian government. The problems within Algeria have spilled across the border on a few occasions – apparently as a reprisal against the Tunisian president for his anti-fundamentalist policies. Ben Ali remains in power, partly by changing the constitution to allow him to do so.

BOURGUIBA

Habib Bourguiba is commemorated in every town with at least one street named after him – and usually a bust or statue too. He was born in Monastir in 1903 and educated at university in Paris. In 1934 he was leader of the **Neo-Destour** (New Constitution) **Party** which was outlawed by the French government. Bourguiba was imprisoned for his political activities on several occasions, including by the Germans in 1942. After the War, he continued to campaign for independence and was arrested and imprisoned once again. Eventually, he negotiated an agreement for Tunisian autonomy which led to independence in 1956. He became president (later president for life) and was the **Father of the Nation**. His long rule ended in 1987 when, at the great age of 84, he was forced to retire. The ousting of Bourguiba is referred to simply as 'the Change'. He lived on under house arrest until his death in 2000 and is still widely revered.

GOVERNMENT AND ECONOMY

Tunisia is an independent **republic** headed by an elected **president** who is head of state and commander in chief of the army. The constitution states that the president must be a **Muslim** and is to be elected for a term of five years. No more than five consecutive terms are permitted.

The administration of the country is carried out through the **National Assembly**, which comprises 182 elected members who serve for five years. Local government is carried out through 24 **Governorates**, the governor of which is appointed by the president. In August 2005 a second-tier legislative chamber, the **Chamber of Advisors**, was inaugurated.

Agriculture

Since ancient times Tunisia has grown a huge variety of crops both for domestic consumption and export. The northern and central areas produce **wheat**, **pulses** and **beans** as well as **melons** and **citrus fruit**. **Vineyards** were planted by the Phoenicians and wine-making is still an important industry, although these days Californian varieties are cultivated. **Tomatoes**, **potatoes** and **red peppers** were introduced by the Spanish from the Americas and are important ingredients for Tunisian cooking today.

The Cap Bon peninsula boasts **mandarins**, **oranges**, **grapefruit**, **strawberries**, **apricots** and **peaches**. In the oases of the south, **dates** – including the fine Deglet Nour variety – are the main crop, though small **bananas** with an intense, sweet flavour are also produced.

Mining and Oil

Although not as rich in oil as Libya and Algeria, Tunisia does have several **large oil deposits** and oil is still a significant industry for the country. Output is approximately 76,000 barrels per day, and there are six main producing areas and several minor fields. The main ones are:

OLIVES

Perfectly suited to the hot, dry Mediterranean climate, the olive, *Olea europaea*, is cultivated for its fruit. Native to the eastern Mediterranean, it is picked both for **eating** and for its delicious **oil**. It contains about 20% oil, the best of which is cold-pressed. Further oil is extracted using heat but is not as good. The olive can be eaten either unripe (green) or ripe (black). The ripe olives are, in fact, blue when they are picked but turn black in the picking process. The **hard wood** of an unproductive tree is prized by cabinet makers and woodworkers.

Al Borma, Ashtart, Belli, Ezzaouia, MDL (Makhrouga, Dabbech and Laarich) and Tazerka. Some new deposits have been discovered in the Cap Bon area and some fields lie across the border with Libya. It is hoped that one day these will be exploited jointly. At the moment, oil export accounts for 20% of Tunisia's foreign exports. The main mining products are **phosphates**, of which Tunisia is one of the world's major producers, while other mining products include **natural gas**, **iron ore**, **lead**, **zinc** and **salt**.

Tourism

Although Tunisia has a mixed economy, tourism is the most important earner of foreign currency. With its endless sand beaches, Roman and Punic ruins and attractive whitewashed towns and villages, Tunisia is determined to exploit its **natural resources**. Over six million foreign visitors arrive in Tunisia every year.

Since the mid-1990s, the government has been increasingly developing the **desert areas** for tourism. Ambitious golf resorts and luxury hotels have been built in order to lure tourists away from the coastal resorts.

In recent years, investors from the Gulf states and elsewhere in the Middle East have poured money into major infrastructure projects, including a new international airport at Enfidha (built with Turkish money and planned to be the largest in Africa, opening in 2009), a new marina at Bizerte, a 'cultural city' near the Tunis waterfront, and (announced in May 2009) the world's third-largest spa resort at Monastir.

Opposite: *Chillies, an important ingredient of Tunisian cuisine, are grown in abundance on the fertile hills of Cap Bon, then sold fresh or dried in the markets.*
Left: *Tunisia is blessed with endless sand beaches and good hotels, catering for all kinds of tourists from families to couples seeking a romantic getaway.*

CALLS TO PRAYER

Most Tunisians are relaxed about their religion, but are still devout. Visitors staying in Tunisian communities soon become accustomed to hearing the **muezzin** of the village or neighbourhood mosque calling the faithful to prayer (*salat*) at dawn, midday, mid-afternoon, sunset and two hours after sunset. However, those staying in purpose-built resort areas such as Port el-Kantaoui may never hear this sonorous sound – which these days usually issues from loud-speakers atop each minaret, not from the muezzin's unassisted lungs.

It is not necessary for a Muslim to attend a **mosque** at all prayer times, only at mid-day on Friday. At other times, the prayers can be performed anywhere. Ritual **washing** precedes the prayer and a Muslim must cleanse his or her face, mouth, hands and feet. For the prayer itself the Muslim must stand on **clean ground** (a carpet for example) and face **Mecca**.

THE PEOPLE

The population of Tunisia is around 10 million, with a quarter of that number under 14 years of age. The extreme youth of the population is immediately apparent even to a casual observer, and children abound everywhere. However, the trend for large families has changed over the last few decades and **population growth** is now pegged at a steady and manageable 1% per annum. The country's **population density** is the highest in North Africa, with most of the people living on or near the coast and over half living in urban areas. By comparison, the interior of the country is very sparsely populated.

Ethnically, Tunisians are largely a mixture of **Arab** and **Berber**. The Berbers were the indigenous people of North Africa who colonized the area some six thousand years ago and comprised most of the population prior to the Arab conquest in the 7th century. Some isolated pockets of ethnic Berbers still exist, but most have intermarried over the centuries. Most Tunisians regard themselves as Arab both culturally and by ancestry.

Although the shift from rural to urban living during the last few decades has changed the face of Tunisian society, there is still a deep regard for **cultural traditions**, mostly kept alive by the numerous festivals which take place throughout the year. Away from the cities and the main tourism centres along the coast, life still centres around traditional close-knit families and small-scale rural agriculture.

The character of modern Tunisia is open and friendly. Tunisians are used to large numbers of foreign visitors in their midst and are generally tolerant of the ways of tourists. In the remoter parts of the country, though, people are more conservative in their behaviour.

Left: The vivid costume of a local Berber woman at a country market stands out from the crowd – the Berbers have always preferred bright colours, unlike the all-enveloping white of city women.

Opposite: Café life is an important part of the social scene: hours can pass catching up with the gossip over cups of tea or coffee.

Language

The official language of Tunisia is **Arabic** but many Tunisians speak fluent **French** – a legacy of colonial days – and **English** and **German** are widely understood in the tourist areas.

Arabic is a Semitic language brought to North Africa during the 7th century. It is the language of the **Koran**, the religious text of **Islam**. Its beautiful, flowing script can be seen on many religious monuments throughout the country and is often used as a decorative element in everything from architecture to pottery. Arabic script is written from right to left and contains no written vowels. For this reason, many non-Arabic speakers find it quite hard to decipher.

In a few remote areas in the south, the **Berber language** – known as *Tifinagh* – is still spoken. This archaic language is not related to Arabic and few people can still speak, let alone write, it.

THE ARABIC LANGUAGE

Arabic is a **Semitic** language related to **Hebrew** and **Aramaic** and even to **Amharic**, the language of Ethiopia, although it is thought to have existed as a separate language from 500BC onwards. The earliest Semitic language was **Akkadian**, dating from 3000BC, and from which **Phoenician** sprang.

Today Arabic is the most widely used of all the Semitic languages. It is the mother tongue of some 150 million Arabs. Being the language of the **Koran**, Arabic is also spoken as a second language by millions more Muslims worldwide.

Above: *The cool, tiled courtyard of the Barber's Mosque in Kairouan.*

RAMADAN

The holy month of **Ramadan** is governed by the lunar calendar and occurs about 11 days earlier each year. It marks the month in which the Koran was first revealed. Ramadan is a time when Muslims renew their relationship with God and each other as a community. The fast ends with **Eidh Al-Fitr**, a feast that lasts several days.

Religion

Almost all Tunisians are **Sunni Muslim**, which is the dominant sect of Islam. Islam is the last of the three 'religions of the book'; the others being Judaism and Christianity. Muslims believe in the one God of the Old and New Testaments and in the prophets of the Bible. They also revere **Jesus** as a prophet, but not as the Messiah.

The Islamic faith was revealed to the **Prophet Mohammed** in Mecca over a period of time between 610 and 632AD. This series of divine revelations was written down and forms the text of the **Koran**, which consists of 114 *suras*, or chapters. Learning the Koran by heart is a highly respected achievement among followers of Islam.

Islam in Tunisia is widely but not fanatically practised. It is most in evidence during the holy month of **Ramadan**. This month-long fast follows the lunar calendar and is slightly earlier each year. During Ramadan, Muslims may neither eat nor drink anything during the hours of daylight. They also may not smoke or have sex. The end of Ramadan is marked by a three-day feast.

The most noticeable feature of Islam is the call to prayer five times a day by the muezzin of the **mosques**. This haunting sound evokes the Arab world more strongly than any other. However, the first call to prayer is at dawn and if you are sleeping close to a mosque its charms may wear a bit thin after a while.

Unusually for a Muslim country, Tunisia also has a **Jewish** presence. This has dwindled since the formation of Israel, but there is still a community, several hundred strong, on the island of **Djerba**.

Traditional Customs

Although some of the age-old traditions have survived intact, many others have not. One of the great changes to take place following independence was the **emancipation of women**. In the early 1950s, women were veiled from puberty onwards, receiving very little education and had their marriages arranged for them. In 1960 polygamy was made illegal and there soon followed a programme to educate women. Many new schools were built and, as a result, women now occupy a vital place in the workforce.

Weddings are still great occasions in family life. Celebrations often take a week and usually follow the traditional pattern of separate gatherings in the bride and groom's family homes, culminating in the hennaed bride in all her finery being brought to the house of her new husband.

The importance of the **family** is unmistakeable in Tunisian life. Many generations may live together as one family unit, although in the capital and other main cities it is becoming more common for couples to set up a new home away from the family house.

In the rural regions and sometimes in the cities, **traditional dress** is still worn. The most common outdoor garment for women is the *haik*, usually white but sometimes black with red fringes in the south of the country. This is an all-enveloping cloak or wrap which is worn covering the head. Underneath, the women often wear western clothing, the *haik* being discarded once they are indoors.

Middle-class men usually dress in western clothes, especially when conducting business. Working-class men usually wear a two-piece work suit and the *chechia*, a dark red, brimless hat made of felt. Sometimes the *jellaba*, a long, loose, sleeved gown, is worn. For special occasions, such as circumcisions, a more elaborate costume is worn, some of it highly decorated.

Below: *Raks Sharki, a lively dance, is sometimes performed at weddings.*

Privacy is a key element in the design of traditional Tunisian houses. Walking around the medinas, you are struck by the blank windowless walls facing the street. Even the doors, with their heavy studs, look more like the portals to a fortress than a family home.

The interior is a different story, however. The heart of the house is always the **courtyard**, which is often open to the sky and highly decorated. Domestic rooms lead off from the central courtyard and, in very large houses, there may even be a second courtyard. Between the inner world and the street is a hallway reception area where (male) visitors can be received without disturbing the female members of the household.

In rural areas, many women wear the indigenous dress called a *mellia*. This is a long, toga-like drape, wound around the body and pinned at the shoulders. Like the distinctive pointed straw hat still worn in Djerba, the *mellia* is a direct descendent of Roman dress.

Arts and Culture

The **fine arts** in Tunisia are well supported by the government. There are many **arts festivals** throughout the year featuring traditional and classical music and drama. Perhaps the most celebrated festival in the calendar is the **Carthage Film Festival** which takes place every other year – in even-numbered years – and showcases contemporary African and Arab cinema. Many Tunisian filmmakers have achieved international acclaim.

The visual arts are thriving and are supported by several **galleries** in the Tunis area. Numerous contemporary artists draw upon the traditional way of life for their subject matter. Modern figurative art has only really developed in Tunisia in the 20th century. The French painter, **Paul Klee**, was an early inspiration, painting scenes of Tunisia in the cubist style. Tunisian painting today is often a vibrant marriage of Islamic and western styles.

Opposite: *Deep blue doorways and shutters are traditional features of Tunisian architecture.*
Right: *A bendir player plays in a traditional orchestra at one of the many folklore festivals that take place throughout the year: recitals are popular and the performance can last several hours, as the music is partly improvised.*

Architecture

The overwhelming impression of Tunisia as perceived by visitors to the country is one of blinding white buildings and deep cobalt blue shutters and doorways. The blue paint, which first evolved as a natural insect repellent, developed into a kind of national architectural style. **Embellishments** to the buildings come in the form of the decorative **grilles** on the windows and the wonderful, brightly coloured **tiles**, used lavishly on both floors and walls.

Modern Tunisians still keep many of the traditional elements in their buildings – even using fake classical **columns**, cast from concrete, to support terraces and to arrange around courtyards. In many of the older buildings, these columns are in fact the real thing: Roman columns that have been re-used in Islamic designs. An excellent example of this is at **Kairouan** where dozens of often mismatched marble columns have been used to great effect in the Great Mosque.

Traditional domestic architecture always followed a basic plan comprising an open **courtyard** surrounded by family rooms, kitchens and store rooms. This was the private area where women lived and worked. In larger houses, there would be a separate reception area for male visitors so as not to disturb the women. Public buildings would simply repeat the same basic plan on a much larger scale.

MUSIC

Arabic music is an acquired taste to Western ears, but with the rise in popularity of world music, it is now gaining a wider audience. This music dates from the courts of the early Islamic Empire and it uses complex rhythmic cycles. Apart from the voice of the singer, the most important instruments are the **ud** (a kind of lute), the **darboukah** (a single drum made of pottery), a **nay** (rather like a recorder), and a **qanun** (a flat, stringed instrument). There are serious efforts to keep Tunisian traditional music alive.

Mosque architecture evolved to give the faithful a place to gather for prayers. Again, there is nearly always an open courtyard with rooms around it, providing places for ritual washing, study and offices. The prayer hall is usually open-plan with a **mihrab** – a niche in the wall – facing Mecca and a **minbar** – like a pulpit – which is used for delivering a sermon on Friday afternoons. **Decoration** in mosques can be very simple or extremely elaborate. During the Ottoman era, mosques were highly decorated with inlaid marble, tilework and carved plaster. Rural mosques, on the other hand, are often just whitewashed and decorated with reed mats around the walls.

Crafts

Traditional crafts are a thriving industry in Tunisia, due in no small part to the large numbers of foreign visitors. A natural by-product of the country's huge numbers of sheep is the **carpet-weaving** industry. The pure wool is woven into three basic carpets: the flat-weave **kelim**, **knotted pile carpets** or *mergoums*, which are flat-woven with distinctive geometric patterns. The natural creamy wool is also woven into simple but elegant **blankets**.

Pottery is a thriving craft, especially on the island of Djerba, and either simple terracotta designs or brightly decorated styles can be found all over the country. **Metalwork** is also popular, and copper- or brass-decorated plates and trays are extremely popular as souvenirs. Silverwork is a speciality of Tunisia and the metal is often worked into elaborate mirror frames and boxes.

In Hammamet and Nabeul, **embroidery** is a local speciality, ranging from clothes to table linen. The studios work in coloured silks and gold thread on either wool, cotton or silk.

HORSE RIDING

Tunisians are very keen on breeding and riding horses. The local **Barb** breed was valued by the Romans, Carthaginians, and Byzantines for its stamina, speed and docility and is still appreciated for those same qualities. In Tunisia there are also **Arabian** horses, either thoroughbred or crossbred with the Barb.

To see horses in action, try the **Douz Festival** in November/December and the thoroughbred **Arabian Horse Festival**, held each June in **Meknassy**. There are also many equestrian centres in and around the main resorts which offer opportunities to ride, and accompanied hacks and treks are available by the hour or by the day.

Sport and Recreation

Outdoor sports are very popular in Tunisia. The climate and long coastline make sailing, **diving** and other **water sports** a natural choice. There are 26 ports and anchorages along the coast in addition to several marinas, with others under construction. On the north coast and Cap Bon, diving is becoming increasingly popular. Tunisia boasts one of the best preserved coasts in the Mediterranean and has numerous dive clubs.

Golf has really taken off in the last few years on the coast, in the desert and on Djerba Island. There are now nine golf courses and talk of more on the way.

For less strenuous activities, there are several Thalassa-therapy **health clubs** where you can reap the benefits of sea-water treatment and massage.

SAND YACHTING

The vast salt flats of **Chott El Jerid** provide the perfect venue for one of the more unusual sports available – sand yachting. In its simplest form, it is just a sailing dinghy mounted on three or four car wheels. Instead of a rudder, the craft has a steering wheel and/or pedals. Latest designs are built for speed and are often up to 7.3m (24ft) long and can carry a crew of three. Wind-propelled vehicles have an ancient history. In 600BC, the **Chinese** developed wind-driven war chariots capable of carrying 30 warriors while, in the 16th century, the **Dutch** had land yachts on wooden wheels. Sand yachting gained popularity after World War II and the first world champion-ships were held in 1970.

Opposite: *Undyed sheep wool is twisted on a simple hand-operated spinning wheel – the carpet and kelim industry relies on hundreds of local artisans to spin, dye and weave the wool.*
Above left: *Water sports at Cap Bon are popular with locals and tourists alike.*
Left: *Specialist golfing holidays in Tunisia are big business; plans are afoot to open new courses, some in the desert oases, in a bid to attract more players.*

Below: *No Friday lunch
would be complete with-
out a plate of steaming
couscous; while cous-
cous is not traditionally
an evening dish, restau-
rants in the tourist areas
also serve it for dinner
due to popular demand.*

Food and Drink

While North African food generally is characterized by its
robust spiciness and its interesting textures, Tunisian cuisine in particular displays a degree of refinement which
makes it a real delight for the visitor. This may be partly
due to the **French influence**, though Tunisian chefs clearly
delight in creating quite original and complex dishes
which remain true to the spirit of North African cooking.

The universal staple is **couscous**, grains of semolina
coated with flour and then steamed. This is accompanied
by a spicy vegetable stew and either meat or fish, or sometimes spicy sausages. Pork is forbidden by Islam and the
favourite meat is **lamb**, although **chicken** is also very popular. The Mediterranean provides a wonderful selection of
seafood and fresh tuna is often available in Tunisia.

Starters are delicious and varied, and there are always
several kinds of **salad**. Notable dishes include *mechouia*
which is a spicy mixture of roast vegetables. Another speciality is *tajine*, which is nothing like the Moroccan stew
of the same name. This is an egg dish – rather like a
quiche – which is served cold.

One speciality not to be missed is *brik à l'oeuf* which is
unique to Tunisia. It is a thin pastry envelope containing
egg and other fillings that is then deep fried until the egg is
just cooked and the pastry crisp. There is an art to
eating this without getting egg on your face.

Tunisians are fond of **stews** and the main flavourings
are cumin, coriander, cinnamon, parsley and hot peppers.
The paste called *harissa* is used with most dishes and
imparts a fiery flavour. It is also served
as a first course as a dip with bread and
tuna drizzled with olive oil. One original stew to try is *mloukhia*, which is
made with a thick sauce of dried herbs
and lamb. The result is tender lamb in a
sauce so dark it is almost black.

Tunisia has a range of delicious
sweet **pastries** in both Arab and French
style. The main ingredients in the Arab
sweets are nuts and honey combined

with dried fruits and wrapped in thin sheets of pastry. A very popular sweet is the crescent-shaped *corne de gazelle*. During the date season in winter, fresh **dates** are served at the end of almost every meal or turned into pastries or puddings of various kinds.

Wine and Beer

Tunisia has been a wine-producing area since Roman times and makes some very good fruity reds and crisp dry whites. Names to look out for are **Gris de Hammamet** and **Vielle Magon**, which are the leading brands. The red is particularly recommended.

Above: *The ever-popular local rosé wines, served chilled, go with most Tunisian food.*

Modern wine-producing methods used today have improved the quality enormously. The most important wine-producing areas are around Cap Bon, the area around Tunis, Bizerte and Thibar.

Quality is controlled by the **Office du Vin**, under a system similar to that of the French. The best-known red wines are Magon, Kahena, Coteaux d'Utique, Chateau Mornag, Chateau Thibar and Chateau Feriani, while popular whites are Blanc de Blanc, Domaine de Karim, Haut Mornag and Muscat de Kelibia. Also well worth trying are the rosés: Gris de Tunisie, Clairet de Bizerte and Sidi Rais.

The only local beer is called **Celtia** and is a light, drinkable, lager-style beer. Imported brands are also available. If you are feeling more adventurous, the local spirit is called **Boukha**, made from figs, and usually diluted with a mixer. It is very strong indeed and an acquired taste.

Even in resort areas, not all cafés and restaurants serve alcoholic beverages. Some cafés claim to serve beer, but the unwary patron may discover, after being served, that it is an alcohol-free brew. Finding a shop which sells wine, beer or spirits (even those produced locally) is a challenge even in resort areas.

Fresh **juices** are usually squeezed to order at juice bars or on the street from the juice sellers. They are both cheap and delicious.

FISH AND SEAFOOD

A great temptation in Tunisian restaurants is the freshly caught Mediterranean seafood. The names on the menu are more often than not in French, so here is a useful glossary:

Anchois Anchovies
Baudroie Angler fish
Calamar Squid
Coquillages Mixed shellfish
Crevettes Large shrimps
Daurade Sea bream
Fruits de Mer Mixed seafood
Huitres Oysters
Langouste Crayfish
Loup de Mer Sea perch
Maquereau Mackerel
Merou Grouper
Pageot Sea bream
Poulpe Octopus
Raie Ray
Racasse Hogfish
Rouget Red mullet
Thon Tuna

2
Tunis

Set on the shores of a lagoon where pink-tinged flamingos wade, Tunis – **The White City** – sparkles in the Mediterranean sun. A dazzling mosaic of souks and minarets lie behind the walls of the old **medina** while, outside, the city has broken free and spread wide with its boulevards and parks, cafés and theatres.

Of all the North African cities, Tunis is perhaps the most cosmopolitan, with an easy-going liberal air – a perfect place to make the transition from West to East. It lacks much of the usual frenetic hubbub of a capital city and marches to a slower, more laid-back beat.

Tunis languished in the backwaters of history until the 7th century, and was little more than a small fishing port on the lagoon. However, its proximity to mighty **Carthage** led it to be used as a military base by besieging armies, and after the Arab leader, **Hassan bin-Numan**, dug a canal out to La Goulette, Tunis gradually became an important port in the African trade to Europe.

The **Hafsid era** was the golden age of Tunis and during the 13th and 14th centuries the great medieval monuments of old Tunis were built within the walls of the medina. The city formed a great marketplace in the Mediterranean; a meeting place for traders from the Muslim East and Christian Europe. **Islamic schools** (*mederessas*) and many of the covered **souks** around the **Great Mosque** were built during this time, as were the traders' *khans*, the **Kasbah** and the **city walls**. By the 15th century, there were approximately 100,000 people living and working in Tunis.

DON'T MISS

*** **Zitouna Mosque:** one of the finest mosques in North Africa.
*** **Shopping in the old medina:** a feast for the eyes and ears.
*** **Sidi Bou Said:** one of the prettiest villages you are likely to see.
** **Dinner at Dar el-Jeld:** a beautiful old house converted to a restaurant – excellent food too.
** **Carthage:** the name evokes its great history, but some imagination is required.

Opposite: *The minaret of the Zitouna Mosque dominates the Tunis skyline.*

Above: *The imposing 19th-century Bab el Bahar (Sea Gate) in the Place de Victoire.*

In the 1500s, Tunis was damaged in the struggle between the Ottomans and the Hapsburgs. The corsair **Barbarossa** took Tunis for the Ottoman Sultan in 1534 but was defeated by **Emperor Charles V** the following year. The city was pillaged and Tunis became a mere pawn in a violent struggle. When the Ottomans finally took control, they added to the monuments of the city in their inimitable style.

Until the time of the **French protectorate**, life in Tunis was largely confined to the medina; outside were only a few slummy suburbs. The French built the vast *Ville Nouvelle* outside of the medina on land reclaimed from the lagoon, introducing some fine colonial architecture. The entire area was laid out on a grid – in stark contrast to the winding lanes of the medina – and the new city housed 150,000 Europeans while the increasingly run-down medina housed 300,000 Tunisians. Following

TUNIS CLIMATE

The capital city is in the northern part of the country and has a typically southern **Mediterranean** climate. Although temperatures can be high in the midsummer months, the weather is comfortably warm for most of the year. Winter can see a surprising amount of rain and thunderstorms.

In the still heat of summer, traffic pollution can occasionally be a problem, but generally the sea breeze keeps the air fresh. The proximity of the salt lakes means that there is a high concentration of UV.

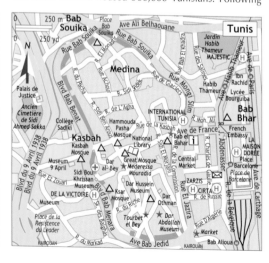

independence, many merchants moved out into the new town, leaving the old medina to house migrant workers. In recent years, however, the government has assumed more and more responsibility for keeping the medina intact.

The **medina** is the old part of Tunis where you will find early monuments such as mosques, souks, *khans* and *mederessas*. It is also in the centre of the modern city which spreads around it. While all the decent hotels and many of the restaurants are in the new city, the medina is free of traffic and has several gates (*bab*) on the periphery.

To the east of the medina is **Tunis Lake** and the port area, one mile from the Place de la Victoire. The main railway station and the post office is south of **Avenue Habib Bourguiba** which runs east–west from the medina to the port. **Belvedere Park** and the **zoo** are to the north and the **Bardo Museum** is to the west.

THE MEDINA

Most walking tours of the medina start at the **Bab el Bahar** (Sea Gate), also known as the Porte de France. This was once the city's lakeside entrance before the land was reclaimed to build the new town. It is here, in the Place de Victoire, that the city seems to assemble in the evening, and watching the world go by from one of the cafés is a great way to soak up the atmosphere.

One of the two main routes penetrating the medina from the Bab el Bahar, Rue de la Kasbah, cuts right through to **Place du Gouvernement** and **Place de la Kasbah**, on the west of the medina, where the government buildings can be found. The **Dar al-Bey** is now the prime minister's office and used to be a government guest house. Almost opposite is the **Kasbah Mosque**, built in 1235, which was built along with the kasbah itself during the Hafsid era. In the same quarter is the **Museum 9 April**, which is dedicated to recording

MEDERESSAS

A *mederessa* is a religious seminary usually attached to a mosque, and was introduced from **Persia** in the 11th century. Its design, based on **Sassanian** architecture of the period, developed into a new kind of mosque, a combination of mosque and study centre, which caught on and spread to many other parts of the Islamic world including Tunisia. The *mederessas* would usually have **dormitory** accommodation built round a **courtyard** for students. There are several examples in Tunis: **Bachiya Mederessa** and **Achouia Mederessa** in the medina.

Below: *A meal in the Dar el-Jeld restaurant is like a visit to the past. The building is an old merchant's house, kept in its original Ottoman style. The food is mouth-watering.*

the life of Habib Bourguiba and the struggle for independence. On this route is the 17th-century **Hammouda Pasha Mosque** with its octagonal minaret built in 1655 and rather Italianate feel. Attached to the mosque is the bright pink marble facade of the **Tourbet (Tomb) of Hammouda Pasha**.

The other main east–west artery through the souk is Rue Jemaa Zitouna. This route has become the main tourist thoroughfare through the medina and, not surprisingly, is lined with tourist shops of all kinds. A short way up this road – on the left – is the **first church** to have been erected in Tunis, dating from the mid-17th century. It became a sanctuary for dissidents and criminals alike, protected by the French and beyond the reach of the Pashas. Also along this stretch are 18th-century barracks, the first of which is **Sidi Morjani Barracks**. Further along is a large former barracks which is now the **National Library**; the entrance is Souk el Attarine.

The Oldest Restaurant

Tunis medina boasts several old restaurants, and one of the best is the **Dar el-Jeld**. Once a merchant's house on the edge of the medina, it serves lunch and dinner to discerning diners. The main covered **courtyard** is the principal dining area, with upper **gallery** rooms reserved for private functions. The food is traditional and cooked by a Tunisian woman whose considerable skills have revived old recipes as well as Tunisian favourites. Despite its splendour, the Dar el-Jeld is not all that expensive – although booking is essential.

The Rue Jemaa Zitouna leads directly to the **Great Mosque**, also called **Zitouna Mosque** (meaning Olive Tree mosque, as it was believed that an olive tree grew on this site under which the founder thought the Koran). The ancient outer walls come from Roman Carthage, as do the many marble columns around the courtyard, and tradition has it that the site was originally occupied by a Temple of Athena. This great building was constructed in the 9th century by the Aghlabids and was a famous seat of learning with over 10,000 students; one of the world's earliest universities, the prayer hall doubled as a lecture hall. Much of the mosque – except for a later addition of a minaret in the northwest corner and a dome over the entrance – is largely in its original condition, but it is no longer a teaching institution since students were moved in the 1960s to the National University of Tunis. Open 08:00–12:00 daily except Friday.

Souks ***

In the medina surrounding the Zitouna Mosque there are numerous covered souks, which traditionally carried out trades such as perfumery, felt-making, spice vending and silk merchandising. Most of these now operate under mixed trades selling all manner of modern and traditional goods. One which has remained true to its roots is the **Souk des Chechias** – found to the northwest of the Zitouna Mosque – and named for the round, brimless felt hats made here. These hats worn by Tunisian men were traditionally dark red but are now produced in an array of colours. Some perfume sellers still have stalls in the **Souk el Attarine** which runs parallel to Rue Jemaa Zitouna. Led here by the fragrances, you can buy a huge variety of essential oils and copies of famous fragrances.

Other interesting souks are the colourful **Souk des Étoffes** with its row upon row of bright fabrics. This souk also houses the **Mederessa Mouradia**, now used to train apprentices in traditional crafts. Nearby is the **Souk el Trouk** where the Turkish tailors made clothes, while leading uphill from Souk des Étoffes is **Souk Sekkajine**, where several of the medina's major carpet shops reside. The exceptionally ornate Palais d'Orient has a much-photographed tiled roof terrace with views across the city and the Zitouna Mosque.

Opposite: *The huge courtyard of the Zitouna Mosque (also called the Great Mosque), with its decorated colonnade, dwarfs the onlooker.*
Left: *Scented oils have been valued for millennia and the perfume souk in Tunis carries on this tradition. Precious oils such as attar of roses can cost many hundreds of pounds for a single ounce.*

IBN KHALDOUN (1332–1406)

This famous and well-loved **historian** and **philosopher** is strongly associated with Tunis, where he was born in 1332 to a wealthy Arab family from Seville. He studied at Zitouna University and served at the Hafsid court for three years. A stormy political career followed, after which he withdrew to write a history of North Africa. This book secured his lasting fame, although his career was not over. He travelled to Kairouan, Cairo and later Damascus where he had an encounter with the legendary Tamerlane. He died in Cairo and is buried in the Sufi cemetery there.

Opposite: *Avenue Bourguiba attracts hundreds of strolling promenaders at dusk.*
Right: *Traditionally women had their own part of the house called the harem – a wax tableau in the Dar Abdallah Museum shows women from a wealthy household in their quarters.*

Rue des Teinturiers **

The old palace of the Dey, **Dar Othman**, is off Rue des Teinturiers in the southern part of the medina, and was built by Othman Dey in the 17th century. It has a stylish facade with a black-and-white marble portal, and a tiled hall leads into a colonnaded courtyard. Much is still in the process of restoration but you are able to peek inside. Currently there are plans afoot to turn the building into a museum of traditional handicrafts. On the same road is the **Mosque of the Dyers** (or Teinturiers), which was completed in 1716 and, true to typical Ottoman style, is lavishly decorated with ornate tiles. This area is now largely given over to fruit and vegetable stalls but there are still a few dyers down the side alleys who use ancient methods to dye bolts of wool, which are draped across the way.

Dar Abdallah Museum **

Also in the southern part of the medina is the Dar Abdallah Museum, an 18th-century palace which now serves as a museum of arts and tradition. It is a beautiful

building well worth a visit even if you are not particularly interested in the exhibits. The tiled entrance hall leads through to a charming courtyard with a fountain, while the surrounding rooms are set-dressed to reflect 19th-century domestic life with various tableaux. One room has a detailed **map** of the medina with all the places of interest clearly indicated on it. The museum is open Monday–Saturday 09:30–16:30.

Close to the Dar Abdallah Museum is the **Tourbet el Bey**, or Tomb of the Bey. This mausoleum has suffered some neglect during the last century but the caretaker is keen enough to show visitors around. Opening hours are the same as those of Dar Abdallah Museum.

The French City

There is relatively little in the way of monuments in the old city, and its charm lies mostly in its stylish colonial architecture, tree-lined streets and open-air cafés. The Avenue Bourguiba is a wide street with trees and flower sellers, and is a favourite promenade sport for Tunisians in the early evening.

The most prominent landmark of the French City is the **Cathedral** on Avenue Bourguiba, a curious mixture of Romanesque, Byzantine and Oriental Baroque building style. Opposite stands the statue of **Ibn Khaldoun**, the great Islamic teacher and philosopher, who was a native of Tunis. Across the way from the cathedral is the Art Nouveau **theatre**: a white wedding cake of stucco and swirling figures which support a curvaceous balcony. The theatre regularly plays host to classical and Arab music concerts.

Central Market

For a change of pace, visit the Central Market in Rue de Belgique where many housewives of the capital do their food shopping. It has a vibrant, colourful Mediterranean atmosphere and the range of **fruit** and **vegetables** has to be seen to be believed. The **fishmongers** bark their prices at passers by while their fish are artfully arranged head up in a rather bizarre still-life tableau. The market is open every day except Sunday.

Right: *These days Tunis has a modern public transport system, including trams and a light-gauge railway serving the city and the suburbs.*

AROUND TUNIS

To the north of the city is the vast Belvedere Park, laid out on a hillside. Green spaces are rare in Tunis and this is the best escape if you want some greenery, as the lower slopes are lush and watered. About halfway up the hill is an 18th-century dome, or *koubba*, which was transplanted here from the suburbs in 1901. At the top of the hill is a spectacular view over Tunis while, below, near the park entrance is the **Museum of Modern Art & Cinema**. In summer this is used for outdoor concerts as part of the Carthage Festival; in the lower section of the park there is also a small **zoo**.

There are few other parks in Tunis. There is the small **Jardin Habib Thameur** off the Avenue de Paris and the **Jardin de Gorjiani** southwest of the medina. The other large green space in Tunis is the old **cemetery** to the south, which provides a peaceful escape.

The Bardo Museum ★★★

One of the world's great museums, this houses a world-class collection of Roman and Byzantine **mosaics** and impressive Punic and Roman **statuary**, as well as an amazing collection rescued from the wreck of the *Mahdia*, a ship from the first century which foundered off the coast. There is also a good display of early Islamic art, and especially impressive is the **tile** collection.

Situated to the northwest of Tunis, the Bardo is a former palace of the mid-19th century. The trip here takes about 30 minutes by road or you can catch the Metro or the No. 3 bus from Tunis. The building itself is rather impressive but most visitors come to admire the Roman mosaics. The collection is so vast and of such a high quality that it is hard to take it in during a single visit.

The designs of the mosaics portray not only grand religious themes but domestic scenes. All of Roman life is depicted here in the finely coloured tesserae. Whereas Italian Romans went in for highly coloured murals in their homes, African Romans preferred their colours on the floor, so this collection is arguably the best there is of mosaic art.

One of the highlights is the magnificent portrait of the poet **Virgil** surrounded by muses of literature and drama; equally breathtaking is the depiction of the triumph of **Neptune**. The themes which captured the Romans' imagination are clearly seen in the smaller panels: hunting, fishing and rural scenes dominate, though there are also still-life studies. Seafood and fish of all kinds were enormously popular subjects all over North Africa and the execution is highly detailed. Open daily except Monday, between 09:00–17:00 in summer and 09:30–16:30 in winter. Entrance is TD3 and there is a small charge for a photo permit.

VIRGIL'S *AENEID*

The Roman poet Virgil devoted the last 11 years of his life to writing this mythological epic, describing the wanderings of the hero, **Aeneas**, from the fall of **Troy** to his military victory in Italy. Aeneas escapes Troy with his aged father on his shoulders leading the way. He assembles a fleet and sails with the other surviving Trojans to Thrace, Crete, Epirus and Sicily before being shipwrecked on the coast of North Africa. **Dido**, Queen of Carthage, falls in love with Aeneas and their story is told in the *Aeneid*.

The style and treatment of the *Aeneid* are derived from ancient **Greek epics** such as the *Iliad*, and it is considered to be the first great literary epic. It was highly thought of in its own day and it later influenced, among others, Alfred Lord Tennyson, John Milton, Geoffrey Chaucer and Dante.

Left: *People travel from all over the world to admire the priceless mosaics at the Bardo Museum.*

Below: *In Carthage the Phoenicians created their greatest city – this villa complex survived the aftermath of the Punic Wars.*

LA GOULETTE

La Goulette on the eastern side of the lagoon serves as Tunis's port area. A new multi-lane motorway crosses the lagoon by a 10km (6-mile) causeway parallel to the TGM suburban railway. Following the causeway, you can see on your left the abandoned fort on the **Isle of Chikli** which was built by the Spanish as an artillery fort in the 16th century and which the Turks later used as a prison. At the entrance to La Goulette is a massive **kasbah** built by Charles V as a defensive position. After it fell to the Turks, it was used as a 'holding pen' for prisoners on their way to the slave market. It last saw action in World War II when the Germans used it as an anti-aircraft position against Allied bombers.

La Goulette today is mostly popular for the many **fish restaurants** which are situated along the sea shore and side streets of the town, giving the place a lively atmosphere in the evenings.

CARTHAGE

The enormous importance of Carthage is not immediately apparent from the surviving **ruins**. The Romans so thoroughly destroyed Punic Carthage, and the subsequent Roman city has usurped so much of the surroundings, that today it is broken up into parcels. If you want to visit the various parts of the site – most of the excavations are in the coastal area of the city – it is best to allow a full day. Tickets may be bought at the Carthage Museum, the Antonine Baths or the Villa de Voliere. Although it is indeed possible to walk the distance, there are no fewer than six **TGM** stations – named after the three main stops: Tunis, (La) Goulette and (La) Marsa – which serve various parts of Carthage. From south to north the useful stations are: Carthage Salammbo (for the Punic ports and the Tophet), Carthage Byrsa or Carthage Demech (for Byrsa Hill) and Carthage Hannibal (for the Magon Quarter and Antonine Baths).

According to tradition, Carthage was founded in 814BC by the **Phoenician** traders, who were constantly on the lookout for a good anchorage; the city thus grew up around the Punic port area. Because it was so thoroughly destroyed by the Romans, no one knows exactly what the first city looked like, but the religious practices of the Carthaginians survived in literature. The worship of **Moloch** and the Carthaginians' notorious child sacrifices were considered outrageous even in the ancient world.

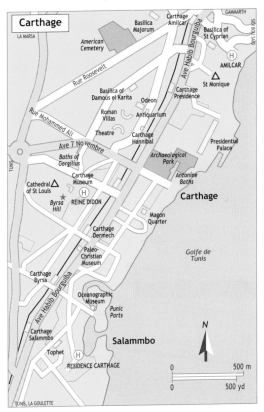

Above: *A solitary statue, dating from the Roman period, stands against the backdrop of Carthage.*

SALAMMBÔ

This novel by **Gustave Flaubert** written in the 19th century is a flight of fantasy based on the mercenary uprising of **Carthage**. It is a tale of sex and violence inspired by the 'human sacrifice' findings at Carthage but, while Flaubert claimed historical accuracy, academics tend to look down their noses at the book. Flaubert's imagination was fired up with his personal vision of the 'mysterious orient' and didn't let fact get in the way of a good story. It has been universally panned as a bad novel – but a very entertaining one at that.

The Roman city was an entirely new town built over the ruins of the old and, by the 2nd century AD, it had become the third city of the Empire, with a population of 700,000 at its height. Later damaged by the **Vandals** and finished off by the **Arabs**, Carthage continued in name only and was quickly reduced to a village, its stones pillaged to build the new city of Tunis and the Great Mosque of Kairouan.

Above: *In its heyday this Phoenician port would have held a hundred or more trading vessels; today the harbour is partly silted up.*

Tophet *

Near the Punic harbour at the southern end of Carthage is Tophet. The discovery of this **Punic burial ground** in 1921 caused a stir, for in the terracotta burial urns were the burned remains of children, giving weight to the theory of child sacrifice. The other name for Tophet is the **Sanctuary of Tanit** (the Punic female deity) who was long known to have been associated with animal sacrifice. However, there is not much to see here and it is only for the dedicated archaeologist.

Punic Ports and Oceanographic Museum *

The **two harbours** are not visually impressive and some imagination may be needed to get an idea of their structure. Historically, though, they are the reason for the existence of Carthage and its subsequent prosperity and, at their peak, the harbours held a fleet of about 220 warships. The island in the middle was the site of the naval headquarters.

On the island now is the **Oceanographic Museum** which houses a collection of fish and other nautical bits and pieces. Open Tuesday–Saturday 10:00–13:00 and 15:00–18:00, and Sunday 10:00–18:00.

Byrsa Hill **

The hill, which was the site of the **acropolis** of Carthage, is surmounted by the late 19th-century **Cathedral of St Louis**, named after the 13th-century French king who died at Carthage during a siege against the Hafsid ruler Al-Mustansir.

The Romans inadvertently saved what are now the best Punic remains in Carthage by levelling off the top of the hill – in order to erect their own buildings – and covering the houses on the hillside with protective rubble. Recent excavations have uncovered these rare examples of **Punic houses**.

The **Carthage Museum** is behind the cathedral on the top of the hill and has a good collection of Punic artefacts including a pair of 4th-century-BC carved marble sarcophagi of a priest and priestess. Open daily from 08:00–19:00 in summer and 08:30–15:00 in winter.

On the west side of the hill are the ruins of an **amphitheatre** where the saints Perpetua and Felicity met their grisly end in the arena in 203AD, the one gored by a heifer and the other killed by a gladiator's sword. In its heyday, this was the largest amphitheatre in North Africa. Nearby are the remains of some **Roman cisterns**.

The Theatre and Villas *

The **theatre** has been completely restored as a venue for the Carthage Festival and bears hardly any resemblance to the original. Although likely to be a major disappointment to purists, it fulfils its role admirably during the festival season.

Nearby is a park which boasts excavated **Roman villas** with some lovely mosaic pavements, broken statues and sarcophagi. To the north of the site are the remains of the odeon (covered theatre).

Below: *The 19th-century Cathedral of St Louis overlooks a section of ruined Punic Carthage.*

Right: *The remains of the Antonine Baths and Magon Quarter are among the most visually interesting parts of Carthage.*

Antonine Baths and Magon Quarter **

The **bath complex**, dating from the middle of the 1st century AD, is perhaps the most visually interesting part of Carthage. The baths were once the largest in the Roman world, covering 3.5ha (9 acres), though all that is visible today are the lower levels – the works – which would once have been lavishly decorated with mosaics and statues. The main swimming pool is Olympic-size and there are many other smaller baths in the complex. A couple of blocks away is an area called the Magon Quarter which has been excavated down to the Punic level. This has revealed mainly **Punic villas** and there are a couple of exhibition rooms with some artefacts.

The Paleo-Christian Museum has some of the later finds from the site. The star exhibit is a **statue of Gannymede** which depicts the beautiful Trojan youth, who was a cup-bearer to the gods, nursing an eagle. Open daily 08:00–17:00 in summer, 08:30–17:30 in winter.

SIDI BOU SAID

Whenever you see an image of a picturesque Tunisian village, chances are that it is Sidi Bou Said. A famous tourist trap for decades, the village seems to have lost none of its charm. It is a cascading tumble of **whitewashed houses** with bright blue paintwork and magenta bougainvillaea descending down to a small and un-crowded beach. The top of the village has views across the **Bay of Tunis**, as well as a collection of **characterful cafés** and small shops.

Left: *Numerous visitors are drawn to the charming village of Sidi Bou Said, famous for its picturesque houses, characterful cafés and chic atmosphere.*

The origins of Sidi Bou Said started with an Arab *ribat* (fortress) on the top of the hill, built in the early years of Arab rule. The site of the *ribat* is now the modern lighthouse. The village grew up and was named after a 13th-century holy man, **Abou Said Khalafa ben Yahia el-Temimi el-Beji**, thankfully shortened.

The village was, for many centuries, out of bounds to non-Muslims but was 'discovered' in the early part of this century by wealthy French colonists who bought houses and went to great pains to preserve the village. As a consequence, the village is completely unspoiled and unique in Tunisia. It is also, not surprisingly, chic and attractive to artists and writers. Cervantes, Simone de Beauvoir, André Gide and Foucault have all been here – as well as the painter Paul Klee who built his reputation on his work in Tunisia. Today the village's art gallery is well worth a visit.

Crafts are still practised in Sidi Bou Said, most famously the **bird cages** made from elaborate wire and wood which reflect the style of the iron grilles over the windows of local houses. After walking around the village, the ultra-trendy cafés are a good place to sip a mint tea and watch the world go by.

GUSTAVE-HENRI JOSSOT

Jossot, who later changed his name to Abdul Karim Jossot, was born in Dijon, France, in 1866. He became known mainly as a cartoonist and magazine illustrator, and visited Tunisia twice before finally settling in Sidi Bou Said in 1910. Three years later he converted to Islam and his work became more Orientalist in style. He remained in Sidi Bou Said and died there in 1951.

Above: *This small marina and bay near Sidi Bou Said stays relatively un-crowded even in summer.*

BEACHES AND COASTAL RESORTS

Although the centre of town is jam-packed with boutiques and expensive French patisseries, there are several beach resorts within easy reach of Tunis. One of the smartest, **La Marsa**, is also an expensive suburb of the city. La Marsa, with its elegant villas, was originally part of ancient Carthage, when it was called Megara. It later became Marsa Al-Roum (Christian Marsa) after the Egyptian Christian Copts who settled there in the 8th century.

The fine summer palaces built in the 19th century are not open to the public but the town is pleasant to wander around. It has a fine, **green-tiled mosque** in the centre and the famous **Café Saf Saf** which is built around an old, tiled Hafsid well, where the water is camel-drawn and the music traditional *malouf*. But the beach, with its wide sandy sweep and palm tree-lined corniche, remains the biggest draw.

Further up the coast is the resort of **Gammarth**, which grew around a series of bays collectively called The Bay of Monkeys. Local fishermen allegedly gave the bay this name because Europeans swam naked there during the 1950s. The town itself has little of interest although there is a fine view of the Bay of Tunis and Jebel Zaghouan from the **French War Cemetery** on the top of the hill.

South of Tunis there is the resort of **Hamman Lif**, named after the ancient **hot spring**. In the late 18th century, Ali Pasha built a palace here among the palm trees as a summer retreat, but the palace no longer exists.

THUBURBO MAJUS

This Roman city is about 55km (34 miles) southwest of Tunis, near the modern village of Fahs, and makes a fine day excursion from the capital. It was originally a Berber city acquired by the Romans in 27BC. Only much later, however – after a visit from the Emperor Hadrian in the 2nd century AD – were the many fine public **Roman buildings** constructed. Several of the temples and public buildings were later converted into Christian churches, but after the Vandal invasion the

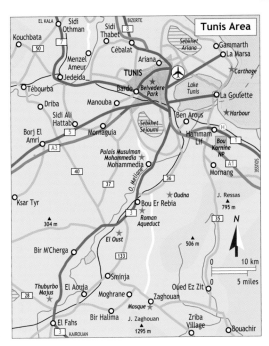

** **Sidi Bou Said**: a quiet, sandy bay.
** **Hamman Lif**: old-world charm by the seaside.
* **La Marsa**: close to the city but not too crowded.
* **Gammarth**: a good beach nearby at Baie des Singes ('Bay of Monkeys').

Left: *The ruins at Thuburbo Majus make a popular day trip from the capital; local families often bring picnics to the site and spend the whole day.*

SIGHTSEEING TIPS

For successful sightseeing in Tunisia it is best to go prepared; it can be very hot and foot-weary work visiting ruins or medinas. Firstly, wear sturdy **sandals** or **trainers** because the ground can be rough going. Essential items are a good pair of **sunglasses** to protect eyes from harmful UV rays and a brimmed **hat** to keep your head and neck cool.

If you are going to visit a **mosque**, dress modestly – no shorts – and women should cover the head and shoulders. Finally, if you are carrying a **camera**, use a protective case to shield it from dust and sun – good ones strap around your waist leaving hands free.

If you are spending more than a couple of hours at an archaeological site, take a bottle of **water** (not soft drinks) with you, as dehydration can be a problem, especially in high summer.

city went into a rapid decline and was used as a shelter by local shepherds, until the excavations this century uncovered the monuments.

The heart of the ruined city is the **forum** which is colonnaded on three sides and dates from 182BC. On the northwest side of the forum is the raised **Capitol Temple**, dedicated to the emperors Marcus Aurelius and Commodus and placed under the protection of Jupiter, Juno and Minerva. On the southwestern side of the forum is the **Agora**, or marketplace, flanked on one side by the **Temple of Mercury**. In the south is the **Portico of the Petronii**, named after the family of Petronius Felix who paid for the construction of the **Palaestra**, or gymnasium. An unusual feature of the city are the two bath complexes: the **Summer Baths** and the **Winter Baths**. One possible explanation for the arrangement is that the water supply to the Winter Baths dried up in summer, necessitating the second series of baths down the hill.

Situated on the road between Thuburbo Majus and Tunis is the sleepy town of **Zaghouan**. Almost alpine in its greenery and gushing **springs**, Zaghouan used to supply Carthage with water. The remains of the 132km (82 miles) **aqueduct** can be seen at a few places on the road back to Tunis.

Right: *Water was the most important commodity in Roman times and aqueducts were built stretching for many miles, such as this one near Zaghouan.*

Tunis at a Glance

Go in spring or autumn; avoid July–August when the weather is too hot for sightseeing.

International scheduled flights arrive at **Tunis International Airport** (tel: 71 754 000, 71 755 000, or 71 848 000), 9km (5.6 miles) from the city centre. Note that the TGM station called Aeroport is nowhere near the airport. A **new international airport** opened in 2009 at Enfidha midway between Tunis and Sousse. **Ferries** from Marseille and Genoa dock at **La Goulette**. **Trains** (including a new, fast, air-conditioned express service between the capital and Sfax) connect Tunis with all points along the coast. **Buses** and *louages* (inter-city shared taxis) connect Tunis with all main towns and cities. Five **Metro lines** radiate from the city centre, where they connect with inter-city trains at Place Barcelone station. For La Goulette, Carthage, Sidi Bou Said and La Marsa, Metro lines 1 and 4 connect with the TGM suburban rail service at Tunis Marine station.

LUXURY
El Mouradi Africa, 50 Ave. Bourgabi, tel: 71 347 477, www.elmouradi.com Modern five-star hotel with rooftop pool in the city centre.
Villa Didon, Byrsa, Carthage, tel: 71 733 437, www.villa

didon.com Dazzlingly stylish designer hotel with just 10 rooms, immaculate service and superb views of bay and city.

MID-RANGE
Hotel Golf Royal, 51–53 Rue de Yougoslavie, tel: 71 344 311, fax: 71 348 155. Large, modern three-star in the centre, not much character but well priced with adequate facilities.
Hotel Dar el Medina, Rue Sidi Ben Arous, Medina, Tunis, tel: 71 563 022 www.darel medina.com Character-filled place to stay on a small street in the heart of the medina, near the Grand Mosque. Good facilities and service.
Hotel Dar Said, Rue Toumi, Sidi Bou Said, tel: 71 729 666, www.darsaid.com.tn The most attractive place to stay in Sidi Bou Said, with an excellent garden restaurant.

BUDGET
Hotel Sidi Boufares, 15 Rue Said Bou Fares, Sidi Bou Said, tel: 71 740 091, www.hotel boufares.com Charming small hotel on quiet side street beside a historic mosque. Conveniently close to Carthage ruins and museum, and within easy reach of Tunis centre by train.

Medina
Café Maure m'Rabet, 27 Souk el-Trouk (no tel). Best of the old-style cafés in the medina.

Sidi Bou Said
Dar Zarrouk, opposite Hotel Dar Said, Rue el Hedi Zarrouk, Sidi Bou Said, tel: 71 729 666, www.darsaid.com.tn Excellent (and pricy), set in a walled garden shaded by lemon trees.
Restaurant Chergui, Rue el Hedi Karrouk, Sidi Bou Said (no tel). Cheap and friendly, pleasant rear courtyard, good grilled lamb, merguez and fish dishes, no alcohol.

Tunisian National Tourist Office, 1 Avenue Mohamed V, tel: 341 717 www.tunisie tourisme.com.tn There is also a tourist information office at place Barcelone station.
Post Office, Rue Charles de Gaulle.
Emergencies
Police: 197
Civil protection: 198
Medical emergencies (CAMU): 71 341 807
Emergency hospitals: 71 578 007, 71 578 346, 71 397 000 or 71 764 066.

TUNIS	J	F	M	A	M	J	J	A	S	O	N	D
AVERAGE TEMP. °F	58	61	65	70	76	84	90	91	87	77	68	60
AVERAGE TEMP. °C	14	16	18	21	24	29	32	33	31	25	20	16
RAINFALL in	2.5	2	1.6	1.4	0.7	0.3	0.1	0.3	1.3	2	1.9	2.4
RAINFALL mm	64	51	41	36	18	8	3	8	33	51	48	61
DAYS OF RAINFALL	13	12	11	9	6	5	2	3	7	9	11	14

3
Northern Tunisia

The northern part of the country is known as **Green Tunisia** and with good reason. The countryside here is surprisingly verdant and lush, and the hills provide a stunning backdrop to the most attractive part of the Tunisian coast. This part of the country has recently been rediscovered for tourism and offers many attractions – not least of which are its superb **scuba-diving** opportunities.

The area is equally rich in history, with several Punic and Roman sites to explore both on the coast and in the **Mejerda Valley**.

UTICA

Named Outiih by the **Phoenicians**, this was one of the first areas in North Africa to be settled by the seafaring traders. Now entirely landlocked, Utica was once a thriving port on the banks of the **Mejerda River** and much of the later city still lies under a 5m (16ft) layer of silt.

According to **Pliny the Elder**, Utica was founded in 1101BC on the original site of a prehistoric settlement, which makes it 300 years older than Carthage. It maintained its independence until the 5th century BC when Carthage forced Utica into an alliance. Later, during the Mercenary and Punic Wars, Utica fought first on one side and then the other. Having supported Carthage in the second Punic War, it changed sides yet again and **General Scipio** was able to use the settlement as a Roman base.

DON'T MISS

*** Sidi Ali El Mekki: reputed to be the finest beach in the country.
*** Tabarka: a beautiful town in a stunning setting.
*** Dougga: the best Roman site in Tunisia.
** Bulla Regia: famed for its unique subterranean Roman villas.
*** Bizerte: a charming historic town and harbour.
** Utica: former capital of the Roman province of Africa.

Opposite: *Of all Tunisia's impressive Roman ruins, Dougga is undoubtably the star.*

Following the fall of Carthage, Utica became the capital city of the Roman province of Africa. Its heyday was in the 2nd century AD, but by the 3rd century the harbour had begun to silt up – always a death knell for trading cities. Utica then went into decline until, by the Middle Ages, the harbour was virtually buried. From the 3rd to 8th centuries it was the seat of a Bishopric, but was finally destroyed by the advancing Arab armies and, for several centuries, pillaged for its building stone.

The site today has a **museum** which boasts a varied collection of artefacts, ranging from coins, jewellery and pottery to a wooden Punic coffin and a large mosaic depicting marine life. Open daily, 08:00–19:00 in summer, 08:30–17:30 in winter. Admission TD2.

Inside the main site, the most prominent monument is the **House of the Cascade**, which was the villa of a wealthy citizen with large ground-floor rooms for entertaining and a pool in the courtyard. There is marble and mosaic decoration still intact. Also on the site is the **forum** and a **Punic Necropolis**.

NORTHERN COASTLINE

Northeast from Utica is the headland called Ras Jebel which has a number of good **beaches**. These are quite undeveloped by the tourist standards of the rest of the country and are often almost deserted. Reputed to be the

NORTHERN TUNISIA CLIMATE

The climate in the north is much fresher than the rest of the country – and a lot wetter too. The summers are dry and hot, with breezes freshening the hilly areas behind the coast. The winters bring torrential showers in the hills; the **wettest** area of Tunisia is at **Aïn Draham**. Rainfall decreases dramatically on the coast and winters there are mild with just occasional rain.

best beach in the north is **Sidi Ali El Mekki** out on the tip of the headland, with an interesting old **Turkish harbour** nearby. The harbour is a relic of the area's former notoriety as a pirate lair, and was attacked and destroyed by Sir Francis Drake in the 17th century. The Ottoman Beys had ambitions for it in the 18th and 19th centuries but the harbour silted up and nowadays only small fishing boats are able to use it. The small port to the south is called **Ghar el Melh** (meaning 'cave of salt'), or Porto Farina. It was once an outpost of Punic Utica, though there is little evidence of this left today. Nevertheless the port, with its **Turkish arcade** and colourful fishing boats, is rather picturesque.

Further along to the west is **Raf Raf**, a huge curve of white sand backed by dunes and then forest. It becomes quite popular at weekends with campers and day trippers, but you can usually lose the crowds further along. There is an interesting walk with spectacular views from here to Cap Farina.

MYSTERIOUS STONE TROUGHS

The **House of the Treasure**, one of the ruined villas at Utica, has a central enclosed **chamber** which has puzzled archaeologists. These appear in several sites in North Africa and all feature stone carved troughs. Various theories have been put forward: animal troughs, bakeries, laundries or warehouses. No one knows the answer. One idea states that the troughs are for portioning out to the servants their rations of food and wine.

Opposite: *Tabarka and its vicinity boast some stunning scenery.*

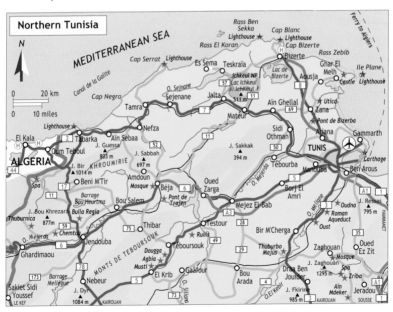

CORAL

Coral reefs come in three types: fringing reef, barrier reef and atoll. The one in northern Tunisia is a **fringing** reef which extends outwards from the shoreline. The reef itself is the accumulation over many centuries of the calcareous exoskeletons of coral animals, calcareous red algae and molluscs. Reefs grow at varied rates, from 1cm to 100cm per year. They are subject to both physical damage and pollutants.

Forming the base for a unique ecosystem, they attract many varieties of fish and other marine life, and make a fascinating place to **dive**. There are several dive centres along the coral coast of Tunisia which offer instruction to novices and more difficult dives for the experienced.

Bizerte ★★

Bizerte lies at the northernmost tip of the African continent and is most famous in recent history as the place where the French dug in and refused to leave after granting independence to Tunisia. The ensuing battle led to thousands of Tunisian casualties, before the French finally retreated on 15 October 1963, a day still commemorated in the Tunisian calendar.

The coastal town straddles the entrance to **Lake Bizerte**, and its excellent harbour has been the cause of frequent occupations and invasions throughout history. It was used as a port by the Phoenicians and they were the first to dig a canal linking the lake with the sea. Later, the Greeks founded a colony here and gave it the name **Hippo Diarrhytus**, which stuck throughout the classical period.

The city was rebuilt by the **Muslim Aghlabids** in the 9th century, but it became a prize in a tug-of-war during the Hapsburg–Ottoman war and suffered accordingly. The old city you see today dates mostly from the 16th century. An **Andalous Quarter** was built to house Muslim refugees from Spain and it became an important corsair base.

Under the French, Bizerte became a naval base; later, during World War II, it was occupied by Axis forces and became a target for Allied bombers. However, the town still retains much of its original character and the attractive harbour area remains the heart of the place.

Right: *The old port of Bizerte is fast becoming a fashionable watering hole for Tunisians and well-heeled tourists – one of those picture-postcard places, it has a special charm of its own.*

Left: *Bizerte's Old Port Café has a long tradition as a good place for locals to while away the heat of the afternoon; now it is also shared by tourists and the new influx of middle-class Tunisians who have moved to the area.*

The **old port** is strung around with blue-and-white houses and the great wall of the old **kasbah**. Nearby is a **fish market** and numerous small **cafés**, which come alive in the evening with tables and cajirs spilling out on the quayside.

On the south side of the **canal** is the recently restored **Fort Sidi al-Hani** which houses a small but interesting **Oceanographic Museum**.

The town **beach** is quite long and sandy and you can hire horses by the hour for a ride along its length. Other beaches within reach are just to the north on Cap Blanc, with the best being **Les Grottes**. To the south of town is the white, sandy beach of **Remel Plage**.

Tabarka ★★★

The beautiful setting of Tabarka is simply breathtaking: the Khroumirie Mountains swoop down to a natural harbour overlooked by an offshore island crowned with a **Genoese fort**. The island is connected to the mainland by a causeway first built by the Carthaginians.

The wealth of the town came originally from the marble taken from the quarries at Chemtou, which was shipped from here to all over the Roman Empire. In more recent times, Tabarka has made quite a decent living from cork production from the nearby forest, as well as agriculture and fishing. The French colonists used it as a hunting resort but, until recently, Tabarka has been left in peace.

CARPETS AND KELIMS

There are both knotted pile carpets and smooth-faced carpets and it is important to know the difference when buying one. **Guetafi Berber carpets** have a long pile, while the **Turkish-style Kairouan carpet** is finely knotted with a short pile (and is far more expensive).

Fashionable and far cheaper are **kelims**, which are made with a combination of knotting and weaving but have a smooth face. These usually feature bold geometric designs. **Mergoum carpets** are smooth and produced by weaving in which the yarn hangs loose on the underside. These are also produced in bright, geometric designs.

Right: *Tabarka is rapidly turning into a heady mix of the old and the new – alongside large numbers of summer tourists, the town still plies its traditional fishing trade.*

BARBAROSSA

The famous pirate **Khayr Ad-Din** (1483–1574) was more popularly known as Barbarossa, meaning 'red beard'. He and his brother, also called Barbarossa, persuaded the Ottoman sultan to engage them on active service in North Africa and, once there, they routed the Spaniards from their recent conquests and stripped them of their new possessions. The brothers thus became the scourge of Christian fleets in the Mediterranean.

In 1518, Khayr Ad-Din was appointed the sultan's representative in Algiers and took the title **Beylerbey**. In 1534, he captured Tunis but was expelled by the Spanish a few years later – only to sack Gibraltar in 1540. His adventurous life is still commemorated and his statue stands outside Istanbul.

The last few years have seen a dramatic amount of tourist development in the area which has come as a bit of a shock to the locals. Nonetheless, Tabarka still retains its attractiveness despite the huge crowds drawn here in July and August.

The main street is lined with cafés, shops and restaurants, as well as the small Hotel de France, where Habib Bourguiba was interned from Tunis in 1952 with his fellow political activists. Their rooms have been kept as a sort of commemorative exhibition. Nearby, to the southwest, is the **Basilica** – in fact a Roman cistern later converted into a church by the White Fathers, and now used as an exhibition and theatre space. Up the hill is another cistern, **Borj Messaoud**, which was converted into a fort by French and Italian merchants in the 12th century.

Situated to the west of the harbour are the much-photographed **Aiguilles**, or Needles, of eroded rock which jut from the water in bizarre shapes. On this side of town is a shingle beach, while to the east is a long stretch of **sandy beach**.

The most prominent feature of Tabarka is the **Genoese fort** on the island, which offers a wonderful view over the town and harbour. The fort has quite a dramatic history. The famous corsair **Barbarossa** surrendered it to Charles V in exchange for the life of the Admiral Dragut who had been imprisoned. The following year Charles V sold it to a

Genoese merchant family who made a living from acting as agents for ransoming captives in Tunis. In the 18th century, the Turks sacked Tabarka and the surrounding outposts and sold the inhabitants of the islands themselves into slavery.

AÏN DRAHAM

This pseudo-Alpine village sits high up the Jebel, 100m (328ft) above sea level, and the drive up from Tabarka should not be missed. As a village, it was created from virtually nothing by the French who wanted to escape the summer heat of the plains and thought it would be amusing to build in a Swiss style. The climate is noticeably cooler and snow in winter is common. The French established the place as a **hunting** resort, an activity which continues today with wild boar as the quarry. The hunting season is from the end of September to February.

For those of a more peaceful disposition, the reason to come here is for the glorious **walks** in the surrounding cork forests and up to the peaks. The paths are well marked for casual walkers and lead to either the eastern peak **Jebel Bir** or the western summit **Jebel Firsig**.

There is also a village women's co-operative which was launched to give employment to local women. The rugs and kelims produced here are sold direct from the workshop and it is an interesting place to visit and watch the carpets being made.

THE WILD BOAR

The wild boar originated in Europe and spread across to North Africa and western Asia, but today boar is rare in Europe, confined to odd mountainous pockets. In Tunisia, the boar lives in the **northern mountain ranges** and is hunted, in season, by foreigners. Pork is forbidden to Muslims, so boar is not usually hunted by Tunisians.

Boars like to travel in small groups and inhabit marshy woodland, feeding on roots and grain. Their lower front teeth grow into large curved **tusks** which can be formidable weapons of defence. A grown boar will charge a man if he thinks he is threatened and could inflict a fatal wound. In Phoenician mythology, **Adonis** – the youth who was loved by both Persephone and Aphrodite – was gored to death by a boar.

Left: *The town of Aïn Draham has been preserved as something of a French architectural folly, with many of its houses looking as if they would be more at home in Provence than North Africa.*

BULLA REGIA AND CHEMTOU
Bulla Regia ★★★

Unique in the Roman world, this site is famous for **subterranean villas** built by the affluent citizens of the city. There is also a profusion of interesting **mosaics** in situ. The hot climate no doubt drove people to build their houses underground, much as they have done in recent history in some Berber villages such as Matmata in the south.

The site was occupied from the 3rd century BC and was a regional capital of the local Numidian kingdom (hence the name Regia). The monuments on view today date from the Roman era and are mostly from the 1st and 2nd century AD.

The city was wealthy, as income was derived from the rich grain-producing areas around the Mejerda Valley. This wealth gave rise, in time, to an indulgent lifestyle and opulence turned to decadence, with Bulla Regia becoming a byword for loose living. **St Augustine** commented on the waywardness of the people in 339 AD when he spent some time in the city. The city's decline began with the Arab invasion and it was finally abandoned in the 12th century.

The site has a small **museum** where you are also able to buy tickets to the site. Once inside, the first building you encounter is the **Baths of Julia Memmia**, the most extensive in the city. It is truly impressive in scale and some of its mosaics have remained intact. The street in front of the baths leads down to the **Theatre**, with a striking bear mosaic in the centre of its stage, while further along is the **Forum**, with a **Temple of Apollo** on the north side and the **Capitol** to the east.

Of all the underground villas, the most impressive is the vast **House of the Hunt** which has a sunken colonnade courtyard. Next

door to this is the **House of Fishing** which, in turn, has a fountain in the basement. To the northeast another villa, the **House of Amphitrite**, boasts quite a famous mosaic in beautiful condition depicting Poseidon and Amphitrite surrounded by cupids.

If you have the time, visit the hill behind the museum – it has several **Neolithic dolmens** dating from a very early occupation of the site.

Above: *Bulla Regia's underground villas kept the Romans cool in summer.*
Opposite: *A bear mosaic found at Bulla Regia.*

Chemtou *

In the same area as Bulla Regia is the **Roman quarry** town of Chemtou. This was the sole source of the highly prized marble known as *antico giallo*. Its rather lurid colouring of yellow veined with red appealed to the Romans' taste – although they were not the first to use it. The Numidians began quarrying the stone here in the 2nd century BC during the time that King Massinissa constructed a massive **altar** on top of the hill (now restored). The marble was first exported to Rome in 78AD and the quarry alone proved profitable enough to support a sizeable town. Each block was stamped with the names of the emperor, the consul and the local official as well as a production number. Later, a factory was set up to turn out finished pieces, small statues and utensils.

The Byzantines also liked this rather gaudy marble and worked the quarry until the Arab invasion. In the 19th century, the works were revived briefly and the **church** on the hill dates from then. The site has open access, and there are a few souvenir sellers with small carvings made from the marble.

MARBLE FOR AFRICA

Be sure to see the remains of the marble factory, under the northern slope of the hill. This was originally a military camp, but the **Romans** turned it into a factory producing marble carvings. It formed an early production line with carvers starting the pieces and passing them on to polishers. These craftsmen used all the small pieces of stone and made statues and utensils.

Right: *The warm, honey-coloured stone of Dougga adds to its attraction as the best Roman site in Tunisia – as this temple shows, the ruins are fairly intact and vividly evoke life in a Roman city.*

CORK

Cork is the outer bark of an evergreen oak tree called *Quercus suber*. It forms a very useful, lightweight material which is also waterproof and impermeable to gas. These qualities make it ideal for use as a **wine-bottle stopper**, but it is also used for wall and floor **tiles**, **shoe innersoles** and, due to its flotation quality, **lifebelts**.

Cork is harvested from trees between the ages of 15 and 20 years, taking care not to cut into the living inner bark. It is then seasoned and boiled to remove tannins. Cork has been used for thousands of years, but it was only after the mass production of bottles in the 16th century that it became an important industry.

DOUGGA

If you only have the time or energy to visit one Roman site in Tunisia, make it this one. It is quite the most evocative and spectacular of the **ruins** on offer. Dougga is situated in a natural limestone basin on the side of the Teboursouk Mountains, with the temple complex on the higher slopes and the Temple of Saturn – with its gigantic columns – standing out for miles around.

Historically, Dougga was neither an important military nor agricultural centre, and its population was not very large, so the fact that it left so many fine monuments is more a testimony to its cultural and religious life. Built on the site of an earlier Carthaginian town, it seems to have inherited a spiritual importance, borne out by the remains of earlier Punic temples beneath the Roman. In fact, it clung to the pagan beliefs of the old world long after most other towns had adopted Christianity.

The **Byzantine** conquest in the 6th century finally finished off pagan Dougga, and the temples were pillaged for stone to build new fortifications. Over the centuries, Dougga dwindled into a small farming village, which remained continuously occupied until the 1950s when the inhabitants were moved to a nearby housing project, **Nouvelle Dougga**, to clear the way for the archaeologists.

The site is 4km (2½ miles) off the road from Teboursouk and is open from dawn to dusk. The first structure you come across is the **Theatre**, which was built in 168AD. Erected at the cost of Marcus Quadrutus, it was one of many grandiose public buildings financed by the wealthy families of Dougga, and could seat 3500 on its 19 tiers. Now restored, it is used every year in May and June for performances by the Comédie Française.

On the hill, high above the theatre, is the **Temple of Saturn**. Its standing columns are the most prominent feature of the surroundings. The layout of the temple is very Punic and it was here that remains of an earlier temple of Baal were found.

At the summit of the hill are remains of the earlier Punic town, the remains of a Numidian tower and a number of megalithic **dolmens**. Further along is the **Temple of Minerva** and the **Hippodrome**.

Back in the central area is a densely packed area of public buildings, among them the **Square of the Winds**, an open space so called because of the compass design on the pavement. Opening off this is the small **Temple of Mercury**, while at the south end of the square is the marketplace.

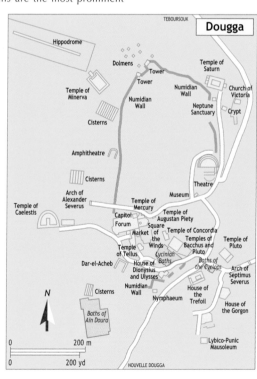

Dougga

Couscous

The golden pyramid of steaming grains called couscous is the national dish of Tunisia and, indeed, of all North Africa. It is made from **semolina** (finely cracked wheat) and moistened and rolled in a fine coating of **flour**. These days it also comes dried in packets. The couscous is steamed over a fragrant **stew** made traditionally with seven vegetables, and meat or fish is also served with it. The steamed grains are piled into a dish, the vegetable stew and its broth is poured on top and the whole thing is crowned with meat. A side dish of fiery *harissa* sauce adds a bite to the dish.

Couscous has become very popular in the West and lends itself to experimentation. It makes delicious **salads** and, as it takes up flavours easily, is a useful ingredient instead of rice.

One of the finest remains in North Africa is the **Capitol**, which, because it is sheltered by the surrounding Byzantine fortress, is very well preserved. A gift to the town from the same Marcii family who also funded the Theatre in the 2nd century, the Capitol looks out over the town and valley below. It is dedicated to Jupiter, Juno and Minerva for the protection of the then joint emperors Marcus Aurelius and Lucius Verus.

To the west are the **forum** and the triumphal **Arch of Alexander Severus**, which was erected in 205AD when Dougga became a municipality. About 100m (330ft) further west is the **Temple of Caelestis** with its unusual semi-circular courtyard. Juno Caelestis was the Roman version of the Carthaginian goddess Tanit.

Right: *The Temple of Saturn is the most magnificent monument at Dougga: people flock to see it at sunset when the last rays turn the ancient stone almost red.*

Left: *The twin domes of the Sidi Bou Makhlouf Mosque in the picturesque town of Le Kef, on the Jebel Dyr, dominate the surrounding skyline.*

One place you should not miss is the town brothel, called, rather coyly, **House of the Trefoil** because of the clover-leaf shape of the main room. The entrance was once decorated with a stone phallus which has now been removed. Next door is the **Cyclops's bath**, named after a mosaic found there, though the main attraction is the well-preserved **public latrine**.

The site also has numerous luxurious **villas** in the residential quarter, the best of these being the **House of Dionysus and Ulysses** – the mosaics which were found here are now in the Bardo Museum in Tunis. Dougga is open daily 08:00–19:00 in summer, 08:30–17:30 in winter.

Le Kef

The site of this unspoilt, picturesque village, situated some 800m (2625ft) above sea level on the Jebel Dyr, has been occupied since Neolithic times and stone tools have been discovered in the nearby **limestone caves**. With views over the plains below, fresh water from springs and shelter in the numerous caves, it has always been a favoured position.

Le Kef was a Carthaginian **fortress** as early as the 5th century BC, but it was later, during the Punic wars, that its name entered history. Known as Sicca, it became a place where the unpaid mercenary army was sent and where they rose up to wage the 'Mercenaries War' against their masters. It was a war of notorious brutality and provided an inspiration for Gustave Flaubert's novel *Salammbô*.

SILVER JEWELLERY

One the most fashionable souvenirs to bring home is a piece of old Berber jewellery. These are often quite heavy and are sold by weight. Some of the more elaborate designs are not very wearable, but the smaller **necklaces** and pairs of **bangles** are much sought after. Large crescent-shaped **cloak pins** and gigantic **earrings** are often reworked into more useful **pendants**. The designs nearly always include the **fish**, a symbol of fertility and luck, and the **hand of Fatima**, daughter of the Prophet, whose palm design you see everywhere warding off the evil eye.

Right: *The ancient synagogue at Le Kef stands long-abandoned, a reminder of more cosmopolitan times in the past.*

FLORA AND FAUNA

More than half the land area of Tunisia experiences a Mediterranean climate and the kind of plant and animal life familiar to southern Europe, with the desert region forming a barrier between the African and Mediterranean vegetation. The most numerous crop plant is the **date palm**, followed by the **olive** (which numbers 30 million trees).

The desert covers about a quarter of the land area and supports plants that thrive in arid soil: **agaves**, **prickly pear**, **thistle** and other thorny shrubs. **Tamarisk** and **oleander** bloom in the wadis, which have periodic water.

Tunisia's wildlife has been reduced in modern times by hunting and the expansion of human settlement. The largest mammal is the **water buffalo** and the smallest the **pygmy shrew**. In the wooded hills of the north, you can catch a glimpse of **genets**, **red foxes** and the **Atlas deer**. In the south, the desert **jerboa** can be seen at night. **Gazelles**, once common, are now seldom seen and even more rare are **monk seals**, now down to one colony in the Mediterranean. These are now protected on the islands of Zembra and Zembetta.

The Arabs came to the town in 688AD and gave it the name Chakbanaria, but it became known as Le Kef (The Rock) in the 17th century.

The main pleasure of Le Kef is simply to wander around and admire the scenery. Nevertheless, there are a few monuments worth investigating. The old **medina** huddles on the hillside beneath the walls of the **kasbah**, and at the centre of town is the spring known as **Ras el Ain**, which has supplied the town with water since its foundation. Near the spring are the remains of **Roman baths**, with an impressive hexagonal chamber. Next door is a **Byzantine church** and, across the road, some ancient **cisterns** supported by dozens of marble columns.

The **Regional Museum of Popular Art & Tradition** in Le Kef is devoted to traditional Bedouin crafts and local life. Open Tuesday–Sunday 09:30–16:00 in winter, 09:00–13:00 and 16:30–19:00 in summer, tel: 78 221 503.

Near Le Kef – 4km (2½ miles) down a side road off the road to Sakiet Sidi Youssef – is the rare chance to bathe in an original **Roman hot tub**, at a place called **Hammam Mellegue**. Of the four original Roman baths, one is still in use, covered now by a *hammam* building. The water is from a natural hot spring which bubbles up at 50°C (122°F) and cools down before reaching the bathing pool. Women can bathe from 12:00 to 14:00 and men thereafter.

Northern Tunisia at a Glance

The north of the country is much less crowded than the more commercial resorts to the south. Even so, it is best to avoid July and August if you want a quieter time. The bathing season starts in **April** and goes through to **October**. When visiting the ruins, go early in the morning before the tour buses arrive (and the light is better then, anyway) or stay longer and take in the sunset.

There are both **bus** and **train** connections from Tunis to Bizerte. From there, you can get buses to the beach resorts and onwards to Tabarka and Ain Draham. There are also *louages* for local destinations and Tunis. From Ain Draham, there are buses to Jendouba and Le Kef. For Bulla Regia, take a **taxi** from Jendouba. For Dougga, take a taxi from the nearest town of Tebersouk, from where there are bus connections to Tunis and Le Kef.

The **roads** are in reasonable condition, and you will definitely need to take a good road map to find the more off-the-beaten-track places. The main routes are the coast road from Tunis to Tabarka, with a turnoff for Bizerte, and the main north–south road from Tabarka to Le Kef. However, most locals use the **bus** services to get around and

there are usually a couple per day from most villages.

Bizerte
Hotel Petit Mousse, Route de la Corniche, tel: 72 432 185. A lovely, small hotel by the beach, with excellent cuisine.
Hotel Corniche, Route de la Corniche, tel: 72 434 744, fax: 72 422 515. Beach-side hotel, formerly a three-star, now unclassified. Cheap, but in need of a face-lift.

Tabarka
Mimosas Dar Tabarka, off Avenue Habib Bourguiba, tel: 78 673 018/728, www.hotel-les-mimosas.com A three-star hotel, good views.
Hotel Les Aiguilles, Rue Hedi Chakar, tel: 78 673 789, fax: 673 604. An old colonial hotel near the beach. Good value; comfortable with air conditioning, TVs and *en-suite* rooms.
Dar Ismail, Tabarka Plage, tel: 78 670 188, www.hotel darismail.com Huge luxury resort hotel on 700m beach, set in 5ha of wooded grounds.

Ain Draham
Hotel La Foret, La Foret, Tabarka, tel: 78 655 302, www.hotellaforet.com.tn Very attractive new four-star hotel in verdant surroundings.

Le Kef
Hotel Leklil, Le Kef, tel: 78 204 747, fax: 78 204 746. With only 40 rooms, Le Kef's

only three-star makes a change from the giant seaside resorts.
Hotel Les Pins, Le Kef, tel: 78 204 300, fax: 78 202 411. Medium-sized hotel; deserves better than its two-star rating and is attractively priced.

Bizerte
Restaurant du Bonheur, 31 Rue Thalbi, tel: 72 431 047. Simple, tasty Tunisian cuisine.
Le Petit Mousse, Hotel Corniche, Route de la Corniche, tel: 72 432 185. Serves some of the best food in the town – at the hotel of the same name.
Restaurant Eden, Route de la Corniche, tel: 72 439 023. Lovely terrace, great fresh fish.

Tabarka
Restaurant Touta, Rue Porto Corallo, tel: 76 671 018. Fresh fish, right by the port.

From Tabarka
Abou Nawas Travel, tel: 78 644 444. A selection of one- or half-day tours to Ain Draham, Bulla Regia and Dougga. The agency also offers a half-day tour of Tabarka that includes a visit to a **cork factory** – a rather popular diversion.

Bizerte Tourist Information Office, Quai Khemais Ternane, tel: 72 432 897.
Tabarka Tourist Information Office, Avenue 7 Novembre, tel: 78 673 555.

4
The Cap Bon
Peninsula

The Cap Bon peninsula sticks out of the coastline like a finger pointing towards Sicily. It forms the northern-most part of the **Dorsal mountain range** and is the undisputed playground of Tunisia. Geographically, it is one of the most attractive areas of the country, with long sandy beaches, and has, as such, attracted tourist development. But once you move away from the coast, you soon find yourself in a landscape of fruit groves and vineyards more reminiscent of Italy than North Africa.

Depending on the season, visitors can often discover small **markets** selling various fresh fruits, vegetables and nuts. Smallholders even set up stall along the side of the road and sell their produce directly to passing motorists. In the autumn, after the grape harvest, the roads are busy with trucks full of grapes, heading for the local winery.

The tourist presence, large though it is, does little to diminish the region's unique character. If you have an aversion to tourists, it may be best to avoid the **Hammamet-Nabeul** area and head for the unspoilt hinter-land. Nevertheless, the hotels along the main coastal strip are nearly all of a manageable, low-level size and keep largely with the local architecture – although a few behemoths have managed to establish themselves. The west coast of Cap Bon is more rugged, less developed and a great place to find a little peace and quiet away from the crowds. The coastline of the Cap also attracts sailors who can explore in peace the tiny rocky inlets. Luxury **marinas** provide a safe haven at the end of the day.

DON'T MISS

*** El Haouaria: visit during the falconry festival in June.
** Hammamet: see its medina and great beach.
** Nabeul: fascinating camel market and pottery.
** Kerkouane: the only true Phoenician town that still exists.
** Korbous: relax in the refreshing hot springs.

Opposite: *Hammamet has become one of the most photographed sights in Tunisia.*

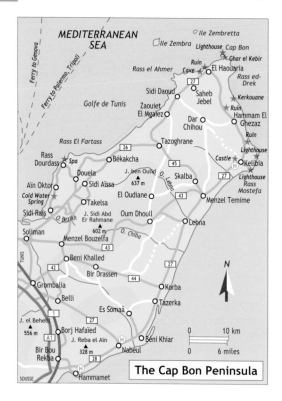

The Cap Bon Peninsula

HAMMAMET

This is the hub of tourism on the Tunisian coast and the largest single resort in the country. The hotels stretch across the sandy bay and now number over 100. In season, the tourists outnumber locals by approximately 12 to one. The entire area is geared to the pleasures of the holidaymaker, and there are all kinds of water sports, golf and riding on offer. As resorts go, it has a lot going for it: the **excellent beach** – the only south-facing one in the country – and a wind shadow protected by the hills behind.

What is surprising is that tourism came so late to this favoured spot. It was in the 1920s that Hammamet caught the eye of a Romanian millionaire, George Sebastian, who built a villa here when it was just a sleepy fishing village. Some low-key yet elegant villas followed and affluent foreigners moved in. Early famous visitors include Oscar Wilde, Paul Klee, and André Gide. World War II, however, put a stop to the party and during the Africa campaign George Sebastian's villa was requisitioned by the Germans and used by Rommel for a few nights.

After the War, Hammamet resumed its role as a holiday resort but it was only in the 1960s that it really took off. The millionaire's residence became part of the **Cultural Centre** and most of the other villas were swallowed up into resort developments. The Cultural

CAP BON CLIMATE

Cap Bon is a rocky promontory and the last gasp of the Dorsal mountains. It benefits from the heat stored up by the Mediterranean and, as a result, **summers** are hot and dry. Breezes cut across the promontory making the area fresher and ideal for sailing.

In **winter**, temperatures on Cap Bon are mild and there is some rain. The sheltered southwestern shore is less windy and has a milder climate.

Centre now holds performances of music and drama during July and August. At other times of the year, it is enough to visit the splendid villa and its interpretation of Tunisian architecture. Open daily, except Sunday 10:00–17:00.

The old part of town still carries on behind the 15th-century walls of the **medina**, surprisingly unspoilt by the tourists. It lies on a rocky promontory sticking out into the sea and is overlooked by the high-walled **kasbah**. In the medina, you can see the 15th-century **Grand Mosque** and the nearby 18th-century Sidi Abdel Khader Mosque. The kasbah has been heavily restored but is worth a visit for the spectacular views across the medina and port from the ramparts. It is open daily 08:30–18:00 during the summer and 09:00–17:00 during the winter.

For a change of scene, try the walk up the valley of Oued Fouara to a small waterfall or, if you prefer, hire a horse to take you up and back along the small stream that flows along the bed of the valley. Horses and guides are available near the Hotel Fouarti. For the more energetic, there is a ruined **Roman temple** of Thinissut, which was dedicated to the Punic god Baal and Tanit, his consort. Some of the statues from here can be seen in the museum at Nabeul.

HAMMAMET FESTIVAL

Held every year from the beginning of July to the middle of August, this festival is one of the most important cultural events on the Tunisian calendar. Concerts take place at the **Cultural Centre** and other venues. Apart from **drama**, **music** and **dance**, it provides a good opportunity to catch a performance by the leading folklore and **traditional dance** troupes, who perform at events all over the world. The setting for the performances is lovely, with splendid views of the sea behind the stage.

Left: *Although nowadays one of the most popular and attractive beaches in Tunisia, it is still possible to see fishermen mending their nets on Hammamet beach at sunset – tourism only came late to this favoured location.*

CAMELS

North Africa without camels would be unimaginable, but in fact camels were quite a late arrival to the Saharan lands. The domestic camel we know today as the **dromedary** originated in **Arabia** as early as 4000BC and, because it was perfectly adapted to life in arid climates, quickly became indispensable to humans.

Camels were first introduced to North Africa as late as the 1st century AD, by the Roman colonists. They quickly became the dominant domestic animal, and were used for **hair**, **milk**, **meat** and **transport**.

NABEUL

The administrative centre for Cap Bon, Nabeul is a great town to explore on foot. Because the local clay is good for ceramics, the place is full of **potteries and crafts shops** of all kinds and you can find just about every possible size and shape of pot here. At the main intersection is a large araucaria pine tree in a giant Ali Baba-style pot; in fact, the tree is planted in the ground – and the pot has been built around the tree.

The clay is also used to produce the most wonderful **tiled panels**, which are a mark of the Andalusian emigrants who set up their workshops here. If you are daunted by the prospect of carrying them home, the panels come apart into single tiles for re-assembly later.

Nabeul was founded in the 12th century, slightly back from the sea which gave it some protection from naval attacks. It developed into a commercial fishing town with a few light industries; apart from the potteries, there are wrought-iron workers and stone carvers. These days it buzzes with tourists combing the many bazaars for bargains. Every Friday there is a **camel market** which closes the centre of town to traffic and sells everything under the sun including, not surprisingly, camels.

Near the railway station on Avenue Bourguiba is a small **museum** which has a modest but very interesting collection of Punic and Roman antiquities. The museum's courtyard features a series of mosaics depicting scenes from the *Iliad*.

Opposite: *These Berber women appear dressed up to attend a local camel market, an event which is popular with locals and tourists alike.*

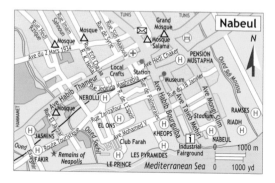

To the south of town is the ancient site of **Neapolis**, which thrived from the 5th century BC to the 7th century AD. It has been partly excavated and the remains of a palace have been uncovered. This palace complex appears to have something to do with the games in honour of the goddess Artemis which were held all over the Roman world and featured athletic competitions. There are also the remains of a factory producing *garum*, a rather pungent fish sauce used liberally by the Romans. This was made from fermented fish and spices, although the exact recipe is lost to us. Neapolis is open daily from dawn to dusk.

Another feature for which Hammamet is well known is its **nightlife**, which can be pretty frenetic during high season. There is a good assortment of restaurants and nightclubs with live entertainment. Expect to be treated to displays of belly dancing, fire-eating and juggling.

FAT-TAILED SHEEP

These sheep are so called on account of the large quantities of **fat** stored around their rump, and highly prized for both their **wool** and their **milk**, they feature all over North Africa. The wool is used to weave **carpets**, the hair being long and coarse. They are perfectly adapted for life in arid regions and represent 25% of the world's sheep population.

KELIBIA

To the north of Nabeul is the much quieter resort of Kelibia, dominated by the striking **Kelibia castle**. The town has a fishing port and boasts some good restaurants which specialize in seafood and serve the unique local **Muscat wine**. The town itself is set back 2km (1¼ miles) from the harbour and is a charming place to stroll around. The town's numerous mosques are decorated with strings of lamps giving it a festive air, and the streets are alive with the activities of various **workshops** producing carpets, metalwork and wood-carvings. Mass tourism is fast catching up with this part of Cap Bon and plans are afoot to build more hotels here.

The port has a **hydrofoil** service to Trapani in Sicily from June to September, which can make rather an interesting excursion if you have

Above: *The port at Kelibia is a great place to try the local fish dishes.*

FISHING

Tunisian waters are home to a large variety of fish and the shallow coastal waters are well stocked. The coastline is 1200km (745 miles) long and different kinds of fishing are practised: **rod and hook**, with a **net**, and with **vertical tackle**. Many resorts offer fishing trips by the day or half day, but underwater fishing requires a **permit** and it is best to contact the Centre Nautique Internationale de Tunisie for information, tel: 71 282 209.

---

plenty of time. The trip takes two hours, but you have to buy tickets from Tunis or Sousse.

The most interesting thing to see in Kelibia is the **castle**. Access is via a steep road which leads up to the entrance. The original Roman fort here was expanded and enclosed by the Byzantines, but then later destroyed. It was rebuilt, and that which is seen today dates mostly from the 16th century when it was repeatedly sacked by the Spaniards. In later times, the castle was occupied by the Axis powers during World War II and damaged by Allied bombs.

The original Roman town of Clupea surrounds the base of the castle and some remains of the original houses may still be seen. Just outside town on the main road is the ruin of a **Roman temple** with some interesting carved decoration, while nearby are the remains of a **villa** dating from the 4th century (although an Islamic shrine to a local holy man has been erected over it).

To the north of the castle mound is a collection of rock-cut **Punic tombs**. About 20 of these were carved from the living rock and descend to a depth of 2m (6½ft).

Kerkouane **

Kerkouane, 9km (5½ miles) north of Kelibia, is the most interesting of all the **Punic sites** in Tunisia. It is thought to date from at least the 6th century BC and remained intact until 256BC when it was sacked by Regulus. The town died after that, so what we have left is a good record of Carthaginian life.

Having escaped the ravages of the Roman Empire, Kerkouane is far more intact than other Punic towns. The town was thought to be the local centre for purple dye production, a secret brought to North Africa from Tyre in Phoenicia. The dye was made from the sacs of murex – a kind of shellfish – and the technique for producing a true purple was a skill which made the fortunes of those able to make it. In fact, it was so highly prized that the colour purple was reserved for Roman nobility.

The site also has a **museum** which houses a collection that includes jewellery of carved semi-precious stones, pottery imported from the Greek potters of southern Italy, small figurines of household gods, and a marvellous wooden sarcophagus cover depicting the goddess Astarte.

The fascinating street plan of Kerkouane reveals that it was conceived and executed to a specific plan, and the houses show advanced plumbing and drainage. The

---

THE CULT OF ASTARTE

One of the most important deities for the **Phoenicians** was Astarte, or Ashtaroth. Her cult was well established in the motherland of Phoenicia long before the colonists founded their cities in North Africa.

She came originally from the **Babylonian** pantheon and was known as **Ishtar** in the early days. Astarte symbolized all the female principles, and was hailed as the **Great Mother**, **Goddess of Fertility** and **Queen of Heaven**. She is best known for the story of her love for **Tammuz**, a story which has come down to us as that of Aphrodite and Adonis.

Left: *Although on first sight not obviously the most exciting of sites, the remains at Kerkouane nevertheless constitute the most intact Punic ruins in the country, having escaped the ravages of the Roman Empire.*

THE ART OF THE *BRIK*

Brik a l'oeuf is unique to Tunisia and is a delightful concoction involving paper-thin pastry, savory filling and a raw egg. The circular sheet of pastry is laid out, some filling placed in the centre, and the egg broken into the middle. The sheet is then wrapped carefully into a semi-circular package and the whole thing is deep-fried until the egg is just cooked but the yolk is still runny. This was devised as a kind of **fast food snack** and, believe it or not, was supposed to be eaten with the hands. The art of eating the brik without getting the yolk all over you was something that needed dexterity and lots of practice. These days it tends to appear on restaurant menus, arrives on a plate and is usually eaten with a knife and fork.

floors show evidence of luxury in the form of marble and blue-glass inlays, while at the centre of the site are the remains of the **sanctuary**. Apart from the main prayer chamber and sacrificial courtyard, there is a kiln room where small terracotta votive figurines were made. Open daily 09:00–18:00 in summer, 09:00–16:00 in winter, tel: 72 294 033.

EL HAOUARIA

This little town is right out on the tip of Cap Bon, with some good beaches nearby – the best being the excellent Rass ed-Drek on the southern side of the point. The town makes a living mainly from tuna fishing but its main claim to fame is the **falconry**. The point of Cap Bon is a corridor across the Mediterranean for migrating birds, especially falcons, and some of the birds are caught when young during the spring and trained to hunt. A big **falconry festival** takes place in June, after which the birds – or most of them – are set free. On Fridays, there is a **market** in town which provides a good opportunity to meet falconers.

There is not much to do in El Haouaria except drink endless coffees and admire the rather pretty blue-and-white town. However, it is worth sampling the local, tiny

bananas which are delicious – this is the only place in Tunisia where they grow.

Nearby Caves and Quarries

A couple of kilometres to the northeast of town is a series of **Roman quarries** and resulting caves. The huge blocks of stone taken from here – originally by the Carthaginians and later by the Romans – were cut out and then shipped to Carthage. The quarrying process left an extraordinary set of pyramid-shaped caverns with daylight shafting down through access holes in the roofs.

About 4km (2½ miles) up the hill from the village and quarries are caves full of **bats**; if you choose not to take a guide, be sure to have a good torch. Hikers will love the view from the top of Jebel Abiod – at 393m (1289ft) it is not a difficult climb – which stretches away to the west coast and the offshore islands of Zembra and Zembretta. These are now part of the Marine National Park of Zemra and Zembretta and are open only to bona fide scientists.

KORBOUS

The main attraction on the north coast, apart from the lovely beaches, is Korbous. Famous since Roman times as a spa resort, the **hot mineral springs** still attract visitors who claim them to be beneficial for a number of ailments. Called Aquae Calidae Carpitanae by the Romans, the springs used to attract regular boatloads from Carthage. In the 19th century Ahmed Bey built a palace near the spring and this was expanded early this century to form the nucleus of a treatment centre, the Établissement Thermal. There are plans to turn this spa into a much larger establishment catering not only for those with ailments but for general tourism. The water itself contains calcium, sulphur and sulphates and is used for the treatment of arthritis, skin complaints and respiratory problems.

A few kilometres from Korbous is the cold mineral spring of **Aïn Oktor** where the foul-tasting water is bottled. Those seeking 'the cure' drink it in vast quantities to relieve kidney ailments and such like.

Opposite: *Cap Bon is the place to go for nature walks and to get away from the crowds.*

The Cap Bon Peninsula at a Glance

BEST TIMES TO VISIT

The weather is at its very best in late **spring** and **early** autumn when the sea temperatures are warm but the sun not too hot. July and August are the busiest months of the year and you will probably need to book ahead to be sure of accommodation during that time.

Throughout the year there are numerous **festivals** and **events**. Some of the main ones are:

March/April – The Orange Blossom Festival at Nabeul.
June – The Falconry Festival at El Haouaria, and the Folk Festival at Nabeul.
July/August – The International Cultural Festival at Hammamet.
September – There are several wine festivals in the villages.

Apart from the main events, there are several weekly **markets** worth visiting: Kelibia on Mondays, Hammamet on Thursdays and Nabeul on Fridays.

GETTING THERE

Hammamet is 1½ hours by **train** from Tunis, but it is on a branch line and you have to change at Bir Bou Rekba Junction. From there, trains connect to Nabeul and Hammamet. From the same junction, you can also connect south to Sousse and Sfax via El Jem.

The opening of the new international airport at Enfidha in 2009/2010 is expected to make the Cap Bon area more accessible to international visitors by attracting low-cost airlines from Europe and the Middle East.

GETTING AROUND

Buses in the region are operated by SRTG Nabeul and serve both the capital and small towns within the Cap Bon Peninsula. The buses are frequent and quite efficient. To get to El Haouaria take a bus to Kelibia and change there. In addition, there are *louage* services which run on various pre-set routes along the south coast and the interior. They also go to and from Tunis. For out-of-the-way places such as Kerkouane, you will need to take a **taxi** both ways from either Nabeul or Kelibia.

WHERE TO STAY

In the main resorts there is no shortage of places to stay – quite the opposite, you are spoilt for choice. In the smaller places, however, there are usually only one or two hotels.

Hammamet
Hotel Sindbad, Avenue des Nations Unies, tel: 72 280 122/162, fax: 280 004. Hotel Sindbad is one of the town's three five-star hotels.

Abou Nawas, tel: 72 281 344, www.abounawas. com.tn This hotel is part of the reliable chain of four-star hotels.
Samira Club, tel: 72 226 185/484/016, fax: 286 100, 226 160, www.samiraclub. com This huge holiday village offers guests every facility under the sun.
Residence Romane, rue Assad Ben Fourat, Hammamet, tel: 72 263 103. Mid-priced, family-operated hotel in the centre of Hammamet with plenty of places to eat and drink nearby.
Dar Hayet, Avenue el Aqaba, Hammamet, tel: 72 283 399. This well-appointed modern resort hotel has excellent views across the Gulf of Hammamet and good services and facilities.

Nabeul
Hotel Kheops, Avenue Mohammed V, tel: 72 286 555/144, fax: 286 024. Large luxury hotel.
Lido Hotel, Avenue 7 Novembre, tel: 72 362 988. Large beach resort, east of town centre.

Kelibia
Palmarina, Beach Road, tel: 72 274 062/063/065, www.palmarina.com Best hotel in Kelibia, three-star.
Hotel Mamounia, Beach Road, tel: 72 296 088, fax: 296 858. A large beach

place with water sports and a nightclub.

El Haouaria
Hotel l'Epervier, Avenue Habib Bourguiba, tel: 72 297 017, fax: 297 258. A small two-star hotel.

Hammamet
Brauhaus le Berbere, Centre Ville, Hammamet, tel: 72 280 082. Good fish dishes are served in this fairly central restaurant.
Sheherazade Restaurant, Avenue des Nations Unies, tel: 72 280 436. Combines dinner and nightclub entertainment, including belly dancing.

Nabeul
L'Olivier, Avenue Hedi Chaker, tel/fax: 72 286 613. Fine French cuisine at a price.
Restaurant Le Bon Kif, Avenue Marbella, tel: 72 222 783. This is one of the best places in town for fresh fish dishes.
La Rotonde, Nabeul Plage, tel: 72 285 782. A seaside restaurant with good views.

Kelibia
Le Relais, Route de la Plage, tel: 72 296 173. Serves reasonable food.
Clupea, tel: 72 296 296. Right on the beach, so be sure to try the seafood.

El Haouaria
Les Grottes, Beach Road, tel: 72 297 296. Mid-range establishment with good local dishes.
L'Epervier, Avenue Habib Bourguiba, tel: 72 297 017. The food is delicious, but very expensive.

There are several possibilities for excursions within and from Cap Bon, and there is no shortage of agencies. Most excursions can be done in one day, although a **desert trip** taking in Sbeitla and the Saharan oases takes three days. There's a shorter trip to the **Berber villages** that only takes one day and includes lunch in a Bedouin tent. Another popular trip is Tunis–Carthage–Sidi Bou Said or, heading the other way, Kairouan and Sousse. A fairly long one-day trip is to El Jem and then down to Matmata to see the **troglodyte dwellings**.
If you want to explore Cap Bon itself there is a full-day trip to many places of interest that are difficult to reach without your own car – including the **spa** at Korbous and also some of the less accessible **archaeological sites**.
In Hammamet there are dozens of agencies all offering a similar service. Try one of the following:

Carthage Tours, Rue Dag Hammarskjoeld, tel: 72 281 926, www.carthage-tours.com
Abou Nawas Travel, Rue Abu Dhabi, tel: 72 282 399.
In Nabeul, try:
Delta Travel, Avenue Habib Bourguiba, tel: 72 271 077.
Salama Voyages, 18 Avenue Habib Bourguiba, tel: 72 285 804 or 287 930.
For independent excursions you may want to **hire a car**. There are several rental agencies in Hammamet and Nabeul:
Avis, Avenue des Hotels, Hammamet, tel: 72 280 303.
Hertz, Avenue des Hotels, tel: 72 280 187.

Hammamet
Tourism Office, Avenue de la Republique, tel: 72 280 423.
Police Station, Avenue Habib Bourguiba, tel: 72 280 079.
Train Station, Avenue Habib Bourguiba, tel: 72 280 174.

Nabeul
Tourism Office, Avenue Taieb Mehiri, tel: 72 286 800/737, fax: 223 358.
Police Station, Avenue Habib Bourguiba, tel: 72 285 474.
Bus Station, Avenue Habib Thameur.
Train Station (*routiere*), tel: 72 285 261; (*ferroviaire*), tel: 72 285 054.
Taxi, tel: 72 222 444.

5
Central Tunisia

The coastal area of central Tunisia, known as the **Sahel**, features a string of seaside towns, most of which are adjacent to some truly lovely beaches. Not surprisingly there is rather a lot of tourist development – but not so much that it spoils the local culture and the pleasure of visiting these historic towns. The interior of the country is predominantly flat with **chotts**, the vast salt lakes which are a major feature of central Tunisia and also other parts of the Mediterranean with low-lying land next to the sea. Because of the flat and low nature of the land, sea water seeps through the sandy soil leaving large areas covered to a depth of only a few feet.

The chotts provide an ideal environment for wading birds, and migratory flocks of **flamingos** can often be seen in large numbers. For humans, though, the vast lakes are not such good news. In winter, they can become treacherous quagmires and have been known to swallow unwary travellers.

Central Tunisia has long been the country's most important olive-growing area and everything from small-holdings to large plantations are dotted with **olive trees**. The area was first settled by Phoenician traders in the 6th century BC, and some of these early settlements have developed into major towns – while others have disappeared in history.

Offshore there are the low-lying, sleepy Kerkennah Islands where **fishing** and, to some degree, **tourism** are the main activities.

DON'T MISS

*** The Roman Amphitheatre (El Jem):** the fourth largest in the world.
*** The Great Mosque (Kairouan):** one of the most important Islamic buildings in the Muslim world.
** The Roman ruins (Sbeitla):** well worth the trip.
** Mahdia:** visit it for its charm and location.
* The Kasbah (Sousse):** on an impressive scale, with a lovely small museum.
* Ksar Hilal:** traditional weaving workshops.
* The Museum of Costume (Monastir):** a fine display of wedding finery.

Opposite: *The Temple of Jupiter at Sbeitla.*

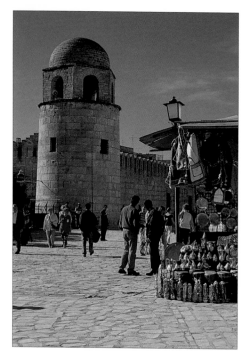

SOUSSE

Sousse is the third largest metropolis in modern Tunisia. Part **tourist resort**, part **industrial** city, it is far and away more cosmopolitan than any other place in the country – apart from the capital. To the north of the city are extensive **beaches** and beach hotels, but the older part of town retains its air of history and contains some fine Arab **architecture**.

Older than Carthage, Sousse was founded by the Phoenicians as a **port** and soon became a flourishing town. A large place of sacrifice uncovered near the Great Mosque indicates the size of the place at the time. It was near here that **Hannibal** landed at the end of his campaign in Italy. As reward for turning against Carthage during the third Punic war, Sousse was rewarded by Scipio and made a free city under the Romans. It later lost this privilege, however, and became the colony of **Hadrumentum**, established by Trajan.

The Roman period was a prosperous one for Sousse, though the city was attacked and badly damaged by the Roman general Cappellianus in the midst of a typically Roman power struggle. Under the Vandals, it became **Hunsericopolis** and, later, under the Byzantines, **Justinianopolis**. The Byzantines enclosed the city behind defensive walls, but after the Arab invasion Sousse was reduced to a shadow of its former self and its citizens enslaved or killed. Renamed **Susa**, it became a new settlement for the Aghlabid Emirs who once again enclosed it behind walls – created from the stones of the Byzantines. In the late 8th century, they constructed the ribat and plans were laid to transform Sousse into a new Arab city.

CENTRAL TUNISIA CLIMATE

The climate of the central belt is that of **desert steppe**. The heat of summer is intense and the humidity is low. The sea along this part of the coast is very shallow and the sea temperatures are therefore warm. Behind the coast, the shallow chotts, in combination with the sea, concentrate the UV light.

This central zone is also known for weather which differs widely from the average. Very wet winters or drought-stricken summers are not unknown.

Most of the Arab monuments seen today date from the 9th century, and include the **Great Mosque**, the **kasbah** and the **ramparts**.

With its new-found importance, Sousse became a target once again and was repeatedly attacked by the Normans, the Spaniards and the Genoese – and even by rival Arab Beys in the 1730s. The Allies in World War II also targeted the city, leading to the need for rebuilding much of the city outside the medina. The French brought the railway and built a new port which provided the infrastructure for today's city.

Opposite: *Sousse is well known for its excellent brassware – here laid out for sale outside the elegant Great Mosque.*
Above left: *The ribat at Sousse nestles in the heart of the modern city.*

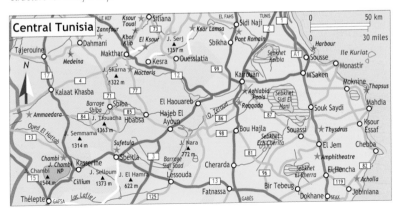

MOSQUES

In the early days of Islam, the faithful were simply called by the **muezzin** and gathered in an open space for prayers. Later, the place of prayer was enclosed and, whereas the direction of **Mecca** was originally marked with a simple **stone**, it was then marked with a niche, or **mihrab**. There are still some examples of these early vernacular mosques in the Sahara.

Mosques became more sophisticated in their design when the **prayer hall** was covered and an open **courtyard** added. **Minarets** made the call to prayer more audible and the courtyard provided rooms for ritual bathing before prayers.

Even in modern mosques, the prayer halls are always simple – carpets cover the floor and there is no furniture save the **minbar**, a kind of pulpit, from which the religious leaders address the faithful.

Right: *The Great Mosque is unique in Tunisia and also uncommon for North Africa's style of architecture. One of the most unusual features is this external staircase leading up to the crenellated walls. This originally had a practical use as the stairs led up to two defensive towers which stood guard over the harbour.*

The Medina **

All the historic monuments and the souks lie within the old, castellated walls of the medina. The best starting point is the Place des Martyrs; the breach in the wall here is a result of bombing in World War II. The **ribat** forms one of the most important of a series of monastery-fortresses built along the coast, which were designed to defend against Christian sea-borne attacks as well as inland raids by Berber tribes. Built by the **Aghlabids**, Sousse ribat was completed in 821AD.

The barbican has four defensive apertures above the gate for pouring boiling oil onto attackers while, inside, the courtyard is very plain and surrounded by cells for the occupants. The watchtower climbs up 73 steps and offers an outstanding view of the whole town. The ribat is open daily 08:00–19:00 in summer, and 08:00–17:30 in winter.

The Great Mosque *

The elegant **courtyard** announces what was, at the time, a new approach to architecture and is almost military in design. No Persian flourishes or recycled Roman columns mar the Great Mosque's simplicity (though some Roman capitals used to support the arches). The main decoration is the Kufic text around the courtyard, while other notable features include its open **kiosk-style minarets**. The Great Mosque was renovated in 1975. Visitors are allowed into the courtyard Saturday–Thursday 08:00–14:00, Friday 08:00–13:00.

The Kasbah and Museum *

This massive construction now houses an excellent archaeological museum on the ground floor, and has the second largest collection of antiquities (after the Bardo) in Tunisia. The Kasbah was built on the site of an earlier Byzantine fort in 859AD, and boasts a 50m (165ft) **tower** named after its builder, Khalef al-Fata,

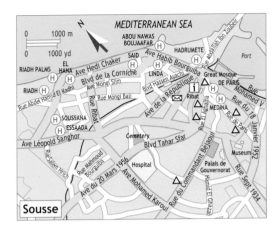

which offers the best view of Sousse – the highest platform is 30m (100ft) above the ribat. It is also one of the oldest towers in North Africa. Unfortunately, the highest level is not open to the public, as it now forms the lighthouse, and visitors have to content themselves with the fine view from the battlement terrace.

The museum has lovely **mosaics** on display, and a magnificent setting among a series of **garden courtyards**. The museum is open Tuesday–Thursday 09:00–12:00 and 15:00–19:00, Friday–Sunday 09:00–18:00 in summer; winter same but closes at 18:00 Tuesday–Thursday.

Souks and Hammams *

In the centre of the medina are the bustling lanes of the souks. This large quarter is a maze of partly covered markets selling all manner of goods. The main thoroughfare runs from east to west from the **Bab el Gharbi** and although the main streets tend to sell tourist souvenirs, a detour down a side lane will show another side to the souk, selling more interesting local produce. There are also many tiny cafés ideal for people-watching.

There are a few good hammams (steam baths) in the medina, but the best is **Grand Bain Maure Sidi Bouraoui** behind the Mosque of Abdel Khader on Rue El Aghalba. Open to men in the morning and women in the afternoon.

Above: *The marina at Port El-Kantaoui.*
Opposite: *The old ramparts of Monastir's medina testify to a rich history.*

The Catacombs ★

On the outskirts of Sousse, about 2km (1¼ miles) to the west of the centre, is a complex of **early Christian catacombs**, some of which have been restored and are open to visitors. The complex carries on for miles through tunnels into which niches were carved for the dead. Some 15,000 graves have been counted. Only a small part of the tunnel system is now open and if you want to view the catacombs you will have to ask at the museum (and be sure to take a good torch). In the same area is the renowned **Sunday market**, which draws people from miles around. There are no camels for sale these days but the event is still one not to miss.

Sport and Recreation ★★

Apart from historic monuments, Sousse's main attractions are its beaches and sports activities. The beaches start near town from the north end of Avenue Habib Bourguiba and all have fine white sand. Most, however, are backed by hotels and apartment blocks and they can become very crowded in high season. All the hotels have a range of **water sports**.

Port El-Kantaoui *

The new resort town of Port El-Kantaoui is about 9km (5½ miles) to the north of Sousse. The town was built from scratch to provide a **large marina**, golf course and hotel resort complex. An attempt was made to create something in traditional style but, apart from everything being painted white, the result is still a brand new made-to-measure resort with plenty of facilities. From the port, you can take a one-day **fishing trip**, or you can try your hand at **golf** on the 18-hole course. There are also opportunities to learn to **scuba dive**.

MONASTIR

The town of Monastir lies 22km (14 miles) to the south of Sousse. This part of the Tunisian coast is densely packed with towns and villages and seems always to have been a rather congested place, even in Punic and Roman times. The advantage is that you can move around from here and visit many places of interest without a long journey time.

Monastir and Skanes have become virtually one place and share an **airport** 7km (4½ miles) south of the town centre. This is the busiest airport for European holiday-makers, with non-stop charter flights coming and going round the clock.

Despite its image as an airport with a resort attached, Monastir is in fact a **university town** and boasts a long and respectable history. It lies on a rocky peninsula at the southern end of the Gulf of Hammamet, and has a small **medina** and also an impressive **ribat** – which has featured in more than one film production, including Monty Python's *Life of Brian*.

Right: *The restrained Bourguiba Mausoleum lies in the heart of Monastir.*

Early Monastir

The origins of Monastir lie in the Phoenician trading port called **Rous Penna**, a name which became corrupted to **Ruspina** under the Romans. During the Roman civil war, Caesar used Ruspina as his headquarters in North Africa and built triple defensive walls around it. The port's strategic importance was not lost to the Arabs, who built a ribat here. The Greek name for these fortified monasteries is *monasterion*, hence the town's name today.

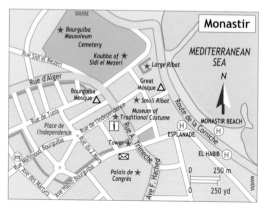

The town became a launch pad for attacks on Christian Sicily and, at one time, counted as the holiest city in Tunisia. Later, during the Turkish period, it maintained an important defensive position and the Beys made it an impregnable **fortress**. It was only during the French protectorate that the city was allowed to dwindle away into a **fishing village**, which is how it remained until the tourist boom.

One of Monastir's recent claims to fame is as the birthplace to President Habib Bourguiba and there is no shortage of reminders of the fact. The **main square** in town, the Place de Gouvernorate, has a bronze statue of the great man in his youth. This is the place to head for in the evening when the place is lit up. No doubt Bourguiba's becoming president of Tunisia helped the development of the town considerably, and one of the most arresting monuments in town is the **Bourguiba Mausoleum**, a 1970s, twin-domed extravaganza.

The Ribat **

The ribat is named after its architect, Arthema Ibn Ayoun, who completed the building in 796AD – though it has seen numerous additions and restorations over the centuries. The **view** from the ramparts is excellent (and even better from the top of the *nador*, or watchtower). It is similar to the one in Sousse and you can supposedly see the tower of Sousse's ribat on a clear day. The former prayer hall on the upper floor now forms an **Islamic Museum** with an interesting collection of Koranic manuscripts and coins, plus some fascinating domestic objects, including early examples of fabric and jewellery. Another permanent exhibition is the **Museum of Costume** near the Tourist Office. It has a display of traditional dress and wedding costumes from all over the country.

The Great Mosque *

There are several other monuments well worth visiting, including the Great Mosque just to the south of the ribat. This was built in the 9th century and added to by the Zirids two centuries later. Another place of interest is the **old**

THE JERICHO ROSE PLANT

When you see an apparently dead ball of tumbleweed careering around the desert what you are in fact seeing is a plant with a strange lifecycle. The Rose of Jericho is known as the **Resurrection Plant**, and for good reason. It starts out as a small herb about 15cm (6 in) tall, with small white flowers. After flowering, the leaves fall and the 'dead' branches curve inwards, making a globular form. The wind tears it loose from its moorings and in this state it rolls and tumbles around the desert. If and when it happens to be blown into water, the branches straighten out again and the seeds are released to start the entire cycle again. The Jericho Rose is related to the **cabbage**; its Latin name is *Anastatica hierochuntica*.

Below: *Fresh fruit and vegetables are sold on the streets of Monastir.*

BIR BAROUTA IN KAIROUAN

The **well of holy water** in Kairouan is at Bir Barouta, a green-tiled building with a blue door in the centre of town. The well is in a first-floor room, with water drawn by a circling camel in a blindfold. The pump room is where you can drink the holy water, which comes up in earthenware jars. According to legend, the well is connected by an underground system of aquifers to the Zemzem spring in Mecca. The building around the well was erected in the 1600s at which time the water was conducted by pipe to the houses in Kairouan.

cemetery which lies, significantly, next to the ribat. There are old *marabout* tombs decorated with tiles and Kufic script.

The Resorts ★

The **beaches** and resort hotels stretch northwards from town, enveloping nearby **Skanes** some 3km (2 miles) away and **Dhikla** just beyond. There is the usual variety of sporting activities available, including horse riding or, if you prefer, camel riding on the beach.

SOUTH OF MONASTIR

To the south of Monastir, about halfway to Mahdia, are two villages of interest.

Ksar Hellal ★

Ksar Hellal is well known for its **weaving** industry and for being the last place to weave silk in Tunisia. The weavers still use handlooms and the results are not only inexpensive but vibrant, original and handmade.

Moknine ★

Just 3km (2miles) away is the village of Moknine, which is well known for its **goldsmiths** – jewellery was traditionally crafted by the village's Jewish population. There is also a **Museum of Local Art and Folklore** which houses some domestic objects, marriage costumes and various Berber artefacts.

If possible you should also try to catch the picturesque **camel market** at the village of Jemmel on Fridays, or the **carpet market** at Ksibet El Mediouni on Thursdays.

MAHDIA

The town of Mahdia is situated out on a narrow rocky peninsula just 500m (550yd) wide that ends in Cap Afrique. Being an important working **fishing port**, the entire town is lovely and unspoiled – despite the number of canning factories nearby which have sprung up due to its proximity to olive groves (for oil production) and sea salt. The **medina** is very picturesque and there is a lovely sand **beach** to the north of town.

Left: *The olive oil industry is particularly important in Mahdia – here a series of woven mats used for straining the oil are rolled up ready for use.*

Mahdia was the site favoured by the **Fatimids** (probably on account of its good harbour and defensible position), and they made it their capital in the 10th century. Most of historical Mahdia was built in 916 to 921 as a retreat for the caliph's family – hence the massive, 11m (36ft) thick wall constructed across the peninsula, with four bastions and a single gateway, creating an impregnable fortress. It was from here that the Fatimids set out to conquer Egypt and take the Caliphate. Once they had succeeded, they moved their capital to Cairo and left Mahdia to fade into obscurity.

Entrance to the old town is through the giant gate, **Skifa el Kahla** – climb to the top of the gate for a view over the old town – and down a 50m (165ft) tunnel. Inside the medina is the **Great Mosque**, which is actually a 20th-century reproduction of the 10th-century original constructed in the typically plain Fatimid style.

Further down the peninsula is the **Borj el Kebir** fortress, a Turkish-built edifice erected in 1595, the battlements of which boast splendid views across the surroundings. Nearby are some Punic **rock-cut tombs** and below these is the old port where a **Roman shipwreck** was discovered early this century. The ship was laden with art treasures, and these may now be seen in the Bardo Museum.

THE ENGLISH PATIENT

The stunning location scenes in the film *The English Patient* starring Ralph Fiennes and Kristin Scott-Thomas were all shot in Tunisia. Wild desert areas near **Tamerza** stood in for the Egyptian Western Desert and the town of **Mahdia** was used to portray 1930s Benghazi. The real Benghazi, in Libya, could not be used as it suffered enormous damage during the siege in World War II and little of its old charm is left today. The film was so popular that many people come to Tunisia just to visit the locations.

El Jem

El Jem is a truly stunning sight on approach. Looming from the flat landscape is the world's fourth-largest **Roman amphitheatre** (of the others, only the Colosseum in Rome and the amphitheatre at Pozzuoli are still intact). When it was built in 230AD, it could easily seat 30,000 spectators, who would travel from all over the region to watch the gladiators fight wild animals, each other or the odd Christian martyr thrown to beasts in the arena. It was meant to be impressive, serving as a message to the locals about the might of Rome. The amphitheatre is open daily 07:00–19:00 in summer, 08:00–17:00 in winter.

El Jem Festival

Every year in July and August, a large international **music festival** is held in the **Roman amphitheatre**, and the setting could not be more dramatic for the classical concerts performed. The Coliseum Symphony Concerts bring thousands of visitors to the town – as the music plays, you can imagine the scene two millennia ago when the arena would have echoed with the roar of wild animals and the screams of their unfortunate victims.

Kairouan

This is Tunisia's oldest Arab city and the fourth-holiest place in Islam (after Mecca, Medina and Jerusalem). Founded by **Oqba Ibn Nafi** in 670AD, Kairouan was intended as a monument to the new Islamic faith and, under the Aghlabids, became a centre for religious and academic studies.

Many tourists come here to perform a pilgrimage and it is said that seven visits to Kairouan is equal to one pilgrimage to Mecca. This specific site was chosen for various reasons: its distance from the Byzantines on the coast and the Berber hill tribes further south, and its convenient situation on a trans-Saharan trade route. The resulting atmosphere is very oriental compared with that of the coastal towns. Large numbers of people (both Muslim and non-Muslim) come here to visit the Great Mosque but, despite the numbers, Kairouan still manages to remain entirely unspoiled. It is actually a rather lively and cheerful little town with a very interesting **medina**.

Even if you are not particularly interested in Islamic architecture the **Great Mosque** is a must, as the sheer scale of the building, with its vast courtyard, has a unique grandeur. Its open space is surrounded with a colonnade of Byzantine and Roman columns – taken from ancient buildings in Carthage and Sousse – which support the Islamic horseshoe arches.

The sacred prayer hall is out of bounds to non-Muslims but you are able to see in through the doorway to the cool, tiled hall. This was the site of the first mosque ever built in North Africa, though the present building dates from the 9th century.

On the outskirts are the 1000-year-old **Aghlabid Pools** which were restored in 1969 and provided a regular water supply to arid Kairouan.

Opposite: *Every visitor to Kairouan comes to see the Great Mosque; though non-Muslims are not allowed into the prayer hall, the splendid court-yard is accessible to all.*
Below: *Kairouan has long been a trading centre for carpets and kelims, here displayed for sale.*

SBEITLA

Very little is known of the early history of Suftela, as it was known in antiquity. These days, Sbeitla is a small **market town** 117km (73 miles) southwest of Kairouan. Only part of the Roman town has been excavated but it is on a par with Bulla Regia and Dougga. Its location means that there are fewer tourists and it can be very impressive in the clear light.

The town appears to date from the end of the 1st century AD, and became a *colonia*. Christianity arrived in the 3rd century and several early **churches** have been discovered. The town found brief fame when, in 647AD, the Byzantine governor Gregorius proclaimed himself emperor here, setting himself up in opposition to Constantine II and moving his capital from Carthage. Unfortunately for him, he was killed that same year in a battle against the Arabs – and this proved to be the end of the road for Sbeitla.

The site has several outstanding monuments. Hard to miss is the **Triumphal Arch** – built at the end of the 3rd century – at the far end of the site. The entrance takes you past two Byzantine forts to the well-preserved **Forum** with its three temples standing neatly in a row and dedicated to Jupiter, Juno and Minerva.

Further along are two basilicas, one with three aisles and a rather grander one with five, which was probably the town's cathedral. Nearby is a small but interesting **baptistery** which is in excellent condition and boasts some fascinating decoration. The small museum opposite the entrance is not very exciting.

MAKTHAR

Set in stunning environs, Makthar – known in ancient times as Mactaris – is worth visiting for the scenery alone. It is located high up in the hills, some 114km (71 miles) northwest of Kairouan in the High Tell. The area is a major corn-growing centre and also produces some olives. The small market town comes alive on Mondays which is market day, but visitors also make the journey to see the lovely **Roman ruins** adjacent to the modern town.

Mactaris was originally a Numidian settlement, dating from around the 2nd century BC, but after the fall of Carthage it became a place of refuge out of the control of the Roman province. It was later incorporated into Africa Nova, extending Rome's boundaries further into the interior. After its destruction following the Arab invasion, the town effectively faded into total obscurity until the French re-established it in 1887 as a market town for the area. It was then that the ruins were discovered.

The site contains a fine **triumphal arch** dedicated to Trajan and some imposing **baths** which are exceptionally well preserved. Don't miss the *schola*, a kind of clubhouse for young men, which is in a beautiful setting. There is a small, good museum on the site, open daily 08:00–18:00 in summer, and Tuesday–Sunday 08:30–17:30 in winter.

Above: *Trajan's Arch, Makhtar.*
Opposite: *This impressive Roman temple in the forum at Sbeitla has been beautifully reconstructed.*

PHOSPHATES

Tunisia relies on phosphate mining for **export** and is the world's third-largest producer. Phosphates are important to the metabolism of both humans and animals, and cattle are often given phosphate as a food supplement. The chemical also has a wide variety of uses in manufacturing: it forms a vital ingredient in **fertilizers** and is added to **detergents** and **water softeners**.

The main phosphate mining areas in Tunisia are in the areas towards the western borders with Algeria. Tunisia produces over 8,000,000 tons of phosphates a year.

Central Tunisia at a Glance

Central Tunisia is the hub of the tourist industry and the main resorts can get very crowded in July and August. For a more peaceful experience, visit in **May** and **June** or **September** to **mid-October**.

Many visitors arrive directly to Monastir-Skanes **airport** and bypass the capital altogether. If you're coming via Tunis, there are frequent **bus** and **train** connections to and from Sousse and Monastir. The train is the comfortable option for this trip and there are several trains a day making the 2¼-hour journey from Sousse (you may have to change for Monastir). By bus, the same trip takes 2½ hours and the fares are similar.

Sousse has many **bus** stations serving the area. You can catch a bus from there to Kairouan, Sfax and some far-flung destinations. There is a bus shuttle going up to Port El Kantaoui frequently. From Monastir, there are frequent services to Sousse and Mahdia and other towns in the area.

Sousse
The choice is the expensive beach strip or somewhere in the medina for atmosphere.
El Hana Beach Hotel, Boulevard de la Corniche, tel: 73 226 900. A lively beach hotel with lovely gardens and the usual beach activities.
Hotel Abou Nawas Boujaafar, Avenue Habib Bourguiba, tel: 73 226 811, fax: 226 574, www.abounawas.com.tn Part of the reliable Abou Nawas chain, on the beachfront but at the town end. Four-star.
Hotel Hadrumete, Place Assed Ibn El Fourad, tel: 73 226 291/292. A small independent hotel with pool in the grounds and heating (rare) in winter.
Claridge, 10 Avenue Habib Bourguiba, tel: 73 224 759. Good inexpensive choice near the town centre.

Monastir
Emir Palace, Beach Road, tel: 73 520 900, fax: 521 823/919. Top-of-the-range hotel, but quite large.
Hotel Yasmine, Route de la Falaise, tel: 73 501 546. Out on the beach road, this hotel is small and friendly and has an excellent restaurant. Some of the rooms have a sea view.

Kantaoui
Hotel Kanta, Port el Kantaoui, tel: 73 683 300, www.kantahotel.com Comfortable four-star standard hotel close to beach and marina, also has excellent self-catering studio apartments, very good value for money. Free Wi-Fi connectivity in public areas.

Mahdia
Hotel Cap Mahdia, Route de la Corniche, tel: 73 683 300, fax: 680 405, www.elmouradi.com Part of the smart Abou Nawas group. Right by the marina with all the comforts you'd expect.
Hotel Mahdia Palace, Route de la Corniche, tel: 73 683 777, fax: 696 810, www.mahdiapalace.com This five-star is the best hotel in Mahdia.

Kairouan
Hotel Splendid, Avenue du 9 Avril 1939, tel: 77 227 522, 230 041, fax: 230 829. A pleasant, traditional hotel with large rooms and a licensed restaurant.
Hotel Tunisia, Avenue de la République, tel: 77 231 775, fax: 231 597. Large, clean rooms with private bath.
Hotel de la Kasbah, Avenue Ibn el-Jazzar, tel: 77 237 301, www.goldenyasmin.com Smart new hotel near medina.

Sousse
Le Lido, Avenue Mohammed V, tel: 73 225 329. A fish restaurant in a nice setting, with reasonable prices.
Le Surfin', Avenue Taieb M'hiri, tel: 73 225 871. Has a selection of set menus always including a catch of the day and plenty of North African specialities such as mechouia and tajines.
La Caleche, Rue Remada, tel: 73 226 489. A simple but smart restaurant, serving a selection of non-Tunisian dishes too.

Monastir

Les Remparts, Avenue Habib Bourguiba, tel: 73 460 752. Local cuisine, reasonable price.
La Rosa, Cap Marina, tel: 73 463 008. An up-market place; local and international cuisine.

Kantaoui

Le Mediterranee, Marina, Port el Kantaoui, tel: 73 348 788. The best of the restaurants surrounding the marina, serving excellent grilled meat and fish dishes. Service is both friendly and efficient.
Le Daurade, Marina, Port el Kantaoui, tel: 73 348 893. The most expensive place to eat on the Marina is very stylish (by local standards) and has an extensive menu and wine list but is perhaps a little over-rated.
The Puca Pub, Hotel Kanta, Port el Kantoui, tel: 73 348 666. Bar-restaurant and sports pub of the Hotel Kanta, with wide-screen TV in an air-conditioned saloon, bar snacks and light meals, tables on a pleasant outdoor terrace and amiable staff.
Platinum, Port el Kantaoui, tel: 20 134 299. The Sousse area's premier dinner restaurant, bar and dance club hosts top international DJs.

Mahdia

Restaurant El-Moez, near the Skifa Al-Kahla, no telephone. Small, friendly, lots of charm. Prices are very good. Try some of the local specialities.

Restaurant de Lido, opposite the port on Avenue Farhat Hached, tel: 73 681 339, 681 476. The restaurant specializes in fish, and is popular with tourists.

Kairouan

Sabra, Avenue de la Republique, tel: 77 235 095. This is a very cheap and simple place, alongside the Hotel Tunisia, and exceedingly popular with locals and the more adventurous visitors as it serves generous helpings of tasty and authentic Tunisian food.
Roi de Cous Cous, Rue Medina, tel: 77 231 337. This restaurant offers traditional divan seating for a truly authentic experience.

TOURS AND EXCURSIONS

Whether you are based in Monastir or Sousse, there are a number of interesting excursions available. A must is a visit to Kairouan to see the fourth-holiest place in all Islam, and to soak up the atmosphere. Tours are also available to Tunis and Carthage and to the south to see Matmata.

USEFUL CONTACTS

Sousse

Tourism Office, 1 Avenue Bourguiba, tel: 73 225 157, fax: 224 261.
Police Station, Rue Pasteur, tel: 73 225 566.
Bus Station, Place Bab Djedid, tel: 73 221 910.
Train Station, Boulevard Hassouna Ayachi, tel: 73 225 321, 224 955 (ferroviaire).

Monastir

Tourism Office, Zone Touristique de Skanes, tel: 73 520 205, fax: 521 219.
Police Station, Rue de Libye, tel: 73 461 432.
Bus Station, near Bab al-Gharbi, tel: 73 461 059, 460 926.
Train Station, Rue Salem Bachir, tel: 73 460 755 (ferroviaire), 461 059 (routiere).

Mahdia

Bus Station, Place 1er Mai, tel: 73 680 372.
Train Station, Avenue Farhat Hached, tel: 73 680 177 (Gare de Mahdia). Place 1er Mai, tel: 73 680 372 (routiere).

KAIROUAN	J	F	M	A	M	J	J	A	S	O	N	D
AVERAGE TEMP. °F	61	64	69	74	79	83	89	91	87	81	72	63
AVERAGE TEMP. °C	16	18	21	23	26	28	32	33	31	27	22	17
RAINFALL in	0.9	0.7	0.8	0.4	0	0	0	0.1	0.5	1.2	1.2	0.6
RAINFALL mm	23	18	20	10	1	0	0	3	13	31	31	15
DAYS OF RAINFALL	4	3	4	3	1	0	0	1	4	4	4	4

6
The Gulf of Gabès

The area known as the Gulf of Gabès stretches from Sfax down to the Isle of Djerba in a sweeping west-facing crescent. The coast all along the Gulf is both sandy and shallow and faces the sun all afternoon. It is not as highly developed for tourism as some of the other coastal areas.

Most visitors head for the popular resort island of **Djerba** or the **Kerkennah Islands** for peace and quiet. On the mainland, the cities of **Sfax** and **Gabès** offer the intrepid visitor a taste of the other side of Tunisia away from the tourist crowds.

SFAX

Easy-going Sfax is the second city in Tunisia and also a major **industrial port**. It is from here that the country's minerals, such as the phosphates mined in the west, are shipped out. The city is also in the centre of a major olive-growing area and oil is another vital export. With its industrial roots firmly established, Sfax has had very little to do with the tourist boom – apart from ferrying visitors across to the nearby Kerkennah Islands. Another reason for the relative lack of interest in the city may be that it has no good beach. As a result, the town has an uncompromisingly Tunisian feel to it and the **medina** is really one of the best to visit for an authentic flavour. The centre of town is a series of elegant, tree-lined streets and squares, although there is a lack of striking monuments; the town suffered considerable damage during World War II.

DON'T MISS

*** Kerkennah Islands: unspoilt peace and quiet.
** The palmery at Gabès: mile upon mile of date palms.
** The beaches of Djerba: miles of sand beaches for lotus-eating.
** Shopping in Houmt Souk: hunt out some special bargains.
* The medina at Sfax: an impressive old town unspoilt by tourism.

Opposite: *The Kerkennah Islands near Sfax offer a world of peace and tranquility.*

The Medina *

The walls of the medina all date from different periods,
but the original was constructed in the 9th century.
Once through the **Bab Diwan** gate on the southern side,
visitors get a glimpse of what all Tunisian medinas were
like before the souvenir sellers moved in. The streets are
very narrow and in the centre is the impressive **Dar
Jellouli Museum** housed in a lovely 17th-century palace,
decorated in the high style of its day with carved wood
and stucco. The exhibits are of costumes and furniture,
and there is also a fine collection of calligraphy. Open
daily (except Monday) 09:30–16:30.

The **souks** in the heart of the medina are a refreshing
change from the commercialism of so many others, and you
can pick up fabrics and spices or perfumes and jewellery
and browse in peace. Lining the medina are many small
cafés and restaurants, one of the most famous of which is
Café Diwan, built into the outer walls of the city.

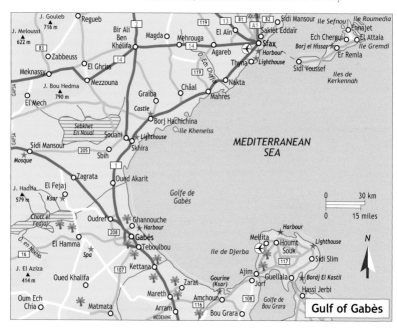

Gulf of Gabès

The avenues and squares of the new town offer splendid opportunities to wander around, and on the main square is the town hall which houses a small **Archaeological Museum**.

KERKENNAH ISLANDS

Sfax is also the jumping-off point for the Kerkennah Islands and, in high season, up to eight ferries a day make the 75-minute trip. The islands lie just 25km (15 miles) offshore but the pace of life is a thousand miles from that of the mainland. The islands are perfect for serious relaxation and doing nothing more strenuous than reading a book for a few days.

The ferries dock at Sidi Youseff on the main island of Gharbi, which is connected to the other main island, Chergui, by a **causeway** of unknown ancient origins, but often attributed to the Romans. Despite their lack of features – the entire archipelago is only a couple of metres above sea level – the islands were known by the Greeks as early as 500BC when they were called Kyrannis, and Hannibal chose them for his exile when he was defeated in the battle of Zama in 202BC. Under the Romans, the islands were renamed Cercina, which transposed into their present name. One unfortunate, Caius Sempronius Graccus, was exiled here and later executed for allegedly seducing the Roman emperor's daughter.

Above: *On Kerkennah pots for catching octopus lie in the sun to dry.*

Today's Islands

The people of the islands today are the descendants of 17th- and 18th-century migrants from the mainland and have in recent history played their part in the independence movement. The trade union leader and political activist, **Farhat Hached**, was born here and his name is commemorated in countless town streets and squares throughout Tunisia.

Visitors to Kerkennah usually head for the **beaches** on the north coast of Chergui, to the resort of El Attaia, where there are low-built hotels and various sports amenities. Naturally, water sports are the main event but you can also go **fishing with the locals** or **ride a horse** along the

SALUKI HUNTING DOGS

These elegant hounds are one of the most ancient breeds of hunting dog. Records dating from 3600BC show the use of salukis – also known as **gazelle hounds** – which originated among the tribes of the **Middle East**. From there they spread throughout **North Africa**. In **Europe**, where they were introduced in the mid-19th century, they were used to course hares, although they are also popular pets. They are very attractive and intelligent dogs with long silky hair covering their ears and long, straight legs; their tail curves upwards. They come in many colours but the shade most associated with salukis is **golden white**, which blends with their desert surroundings perfectly.

Right: *Colourful fishing boats lie hauled up onto the long sand beach at Gabès, an otherwise predominantly modern town.*

shore. The fishing trips are fascinating: local fishermen still use traditional fishing methods using palm-frond fish traps. One of the favourite catches is octopus which is frozen in Sfax and exported to Japan.

One of the few ancient remains on Kerkennah is the **Borj El Hissar**, an old Turkish tower now in ruins, but more interesting are the remains of the Roman fort which surround it. There are still mosaics in situ although the sea has reclaimed some of the buildings and the site has a rather desolate air.

GABÈS

The name 'Gabès' means 'gateway to the south' in Arabic. About halfway along the Gulf of Gabès and known in antiquity as Syrtis Minor, the town is strategically placed on an intersection of the Saharan trade route and the main coastal road to the north. As a result of its position, the town thrived and was particularly prosperous during the Middle Ages.

Its most striking feature is the vast palmery with over **half a million date palms** and countless other fruit trees, while the other main attraction is the very **long sand beach**. The picture would not be complete, though, without mentioning the heavy industry in this area which rather takes the edge off the romantic image: the town makes a living nowadays not so much from agriculture but from phosphates, cement and an oil refinery.

Tourists still visit Gabès in surprisingly large numbers to enjoy the beach and to take a horse-drawn calash around the oasis, where there is also a rather poor **zoo** and a **crocodile farm**. Another way to explore the oasis is by bicycle; these are available for hire and you can do a complete circuit, stopping at places of interest, in approximately four hours.

The town itself is rather modern and not very pretty. The main street, Avenue Habib Bourguiba, forms the principal shopping area, while out on its own to the north is the older quarter of town, called Petite Jara, with an 11th-century mosque.

On a hill in the southwest part of town, the most notable monument in Gabès is the **Mosque of Sidi Boulbaba**, named for the Prophet Mohammed's barber, who retired to Gabès and is buried here. The courtyard is open to visitors and has some fine tilework and Koranic inscriptions. Next door, in the old *mederessa*, is a **folklore museum**.

Excursions from Gabès ★

The oasis villages on the outskirts of the town are well worth visiting for their charm. The most popular, **Chenini du Gabès** – only 4km (2½ miles) to the west – is well known for its fine basket-weaving. On the way are the remains of a **Roman reservoir**.

ULYSSES

Known as Odysseus in Greek mythology, Ulysses was the ruler of the island of **Ithaca** and one of the leaders of the Greek army during the **Trojan War**. The immortal classic by Homer, *The Odyssey*, tells of his epic and eventful journey home 10 years after the fall of Troy, including a stay on Djerba – 'land of the lotus-eaters'. Ulysses appears earlier in *The Iliad* as a brave and cunning warrior, and it was he who brought the heroes **Neoptolemus** and **Philoctetes** to Troy for the final stage of the war. He is also memorably attributed with coming up with the idea of the **Trojan Horse**, the means by which the Greek army entered Troy and destroyed it.

Left: *One way to relax is to take a ride in these brightly painted carriages around the various oases in the vicinity of Gabès.*

Below: *The sponge industry on Djerba dates back a long time.*

DJERBA ISLAND

Lying at the southern end of the Gulf of Gabès, Djerba is the largest of Tunisia's – or indeed North Africa's – islands and is a deservedly popular destination for European tourists. The north coast has a string of **beach resort hotels** along sandy, white shores and the interior has some interesting towns to explore, including the capital, **Houmt Souk**. The land itself is flat and low-lying, covered with palms and olive trees and dotted with dome-topped, white farmhouses and unique fortified mosques. The island was a part of the mainland until the last Ice Age and is now connected by a 6½ km (4-mile) causeway.

Djerba gained a place in mythology when **Homer** immortalized it in the **Odyssey** as the 'land of the lotus-eaters' – the legendary fruit was supposed to lull the eater into a reverie and make them forget about home – and this term has passed down to us as a place of abundant pleasure. **Ulysses** was supposed to have paused here on his journey and his crew were so taken with the place that they had to be physically forced back aboard the ship and wept all the way.

A more certain history relates that Djerba was the Phoenician **Meninx**, dating from the 9th century BC – the name was probably a corruption of murex, the shellfish used to make purple dye, as large numbers of shells have been found here. The Romans later built four cities on the island and it became a rich trading post and port. One of the towns was called **Girba**, from which its current name derives.

Although the island caters for large numbers of tourists, it is easy enough to find a deserted place either on the west coast or in the rural interior, ideal for exploring by bicycle.

Houmt Souk **

The only proper town on Djerba is its capital, Houmt Souk, a place of great charm despite its obvious commercial leanings. The older quarter has a wealth of historic buildings, and some are now hotels converted from old funduqs or caravanserais into modest but attractive places to stay. They are all built on two floors with a central courtyard; in the old days the ground floor rooms were for animals and goods, and the upper rooms the merchants' sleeping quarters. The town has about 65,000 inhabitants, most of whom make a living one way or another from **tourism**. The remainder still carry on **fishing** in the time-honoured way.

Houmt Souk is well worth visiting for, not surprisingly, its **souk** area, where you can buy – among other items – colourful, inexpensive local pottery and woven baskets. Not to be missed is the daily **fish auction** in the souk. The best days to visit the souk are Mondays and Thursdays, when people come from outside to sell their goods.

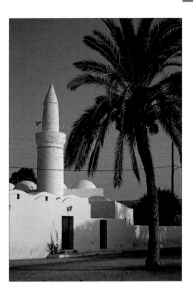

Above: *A local mosque on Djerba – the island's architecture is simple and relaxed.*

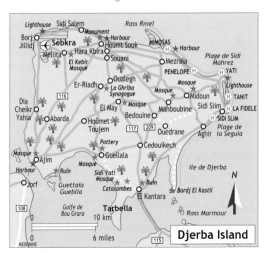

Djerba Island

DJERBA POTTERY

It would be hard to miss the island's most celebrated product. The colourful plates, bowls and jugs spill out onto the pavement along **roadsides** and fill countless shops in the **souk**. There is something for virtually every taste: brilliantly coloured bold pieces alongside more subtle pastel earthenware. Highly decorative are the pierced-work, plain terracotta lanterns which can hang on a wall in the garden or grace a table with a candle inside. The pottery is all at bargain prices and makes a good souvenir.

Right: *La Ghriba Syna-gogue is the focus of an annual pilgrimage – Jewish traditions still hold strong amongst the tiny nearby community of Er Riadh.*

Borj el Kebir *

Just to the north of town, within easy walking distance, is the Borj el Kebir, an old **medieval fortification** which saw heavy action in 1560 when Philip of Spain's armada was destroyed by Dragut's Ottoman fleet. The Spaniards took refuge inside the tower only to be massacred by the Turks who piled their skulls in a great mound inside the tower; it was not until 1848 that their remains were allowed to be buried.

Along the road to the Borj, an unofficial '**Libyan market**' has evolved selling consumer goods from across the border.

Er Riadh/Hara Seghira *

This small town 8km (5 miles) from Houmt Souk is one of two villages on Djerba which is a traditional home to a large Jewish community, formerly known as **Hara Seghira** (little ghetto) and renamed **Er Riadh**. It is well documented that Jews came to Djerba after the fall of Jerusalem in 70AD, but it is thought that the original Jewish settlers arrived much earlier: in the 6th century BC. Others came after Andalucía fell to the Spanish and, at their height, the Jewish population of Djerba was 10 per cent of the total population, but this figure has dwindled in the post-Israel years to a few hundred.

There is a famous **synagogue** near Er Riadh called **La Ghriba** – meaning 'wonder-working' – and every year, 33

THE JEWS OF DJERBA

Djerba has been home to an active Jewish community since the diaspora following the fall of **Jerusalem** to **Nebuchadnezzar** in 71BC – or so it is thought. The community has been established so long that its true history has been lost in time. The community today numbers about 1500 and plays a vital role in the island **economy**. Traditionally, they have specialized in **jewellery** and several small Jewish colonies have sprang up over the southern part of the island. Near Er Riadh is one of the holiest **synagogues** in North Africa, which is the site of a **pilgrimage** every year on 22 and 23 May. The present building is modern – built in 1920 – but the site was supposedly first established in 600BC.

days after Easter, it is a place of pilgrimage for many North African Jews. It is open to visitors daily except during Saturday morning prayer. Dress modestly.

Midoun **

Midoun is the main market town of the interior and is a popular place to visit, especially for its Friday market. It is just 5km (3 miles) inland from the north coast resorts. Every Thursday during the summer there is a display of **traditional wedding celebrations** put on for the tourists. Among other things, you can see camels, dancing and trick horse-riding displays.

Guellala *

In the south of Djerba is the small town of Guellala, known in ancient times as Haribus, which is a great pottery-producing centre – just as it was in antiquity. It is said that there are over 400 **potters** working here and although the range of goods is huge, the local tradition is to make unglazed terracotta amphorae. The local clay is mined from deep shafts, dried and then mixed with fresh water for red pots and salt water for white. These are left for two months to dry before being fired.

MIDOUN FRIDAY MARKET

This uneventful small town really comes to life for the Friday market. As **souks** go, this is the most interesting on Djerba, with all kinds of goods on offer from **traditional** to **modern**, cheap to expensive – although there is also a fair amount of tourist tat. Even if you don't want to buy any-thing, it is a great opportunity to soak up the **atmosphere** of a Djerban souk. Farmers and traders sit beneath their straw hats patiently waiting for a cus-tomer in the hot sun, arguing with hagglers and hangers-on. A vivid cross-section of Djerban society gathers here and it should not be missed.

Left: *Djerba is famous for its colourful pottery, ranging from highly dec-orative to plain terracotta pieces; nowhere is this more in evidence than in the small town of Guellala.*

Gulf of Gabès at a Glance

The Gulf of Gabès region is at its best between **April** and **October** when the weather is hot and dry.

Sfax is on the domestic **air** route from Tunis and there are daily connections. Djerba connects with Tunis about five times a day, but also has direct air routes to many European cities, plus holiday charter flights. **Bus** services run from Tunis to Sfax and to Djerba (Tunis–Djerba takes 6¼ hours). There are the usual comprehensive *louage* services running to all the towns along the Gulf of Gabès and to Tunis. From Sfax, there is also the option of travelling by **train** both south to Gabès and north to Sousse and Tunis.

Sfax
Local **buses** serve the town and outlying villages and leave from a terminus near the junction of Avenue des Martyrs and Avenue 18 Janvier, at the north end of the old town. Otherwise, the **shared taxis** (*louages*) leave from a group of taxi stands along and around Avenue Ali Belhouane and cover routes in all directions.

Gabès
The *louages* station is alongside the **bus** station on the western end of Avenue Farhat Hached. Hire a **bicycle** to tour the palmery; the hire shop is near the Hotel de la Poste.

Djerba
A network of local **buses** serves the towns of the island. They leave from the same bus station as the long-distance buses at the southern end of Avenue Habib Bourguiba. There are two main **taxi** stations in Houmt Souk; one in Avenue Habib Bourguiba and the other in Place Sidi Ibrahim, a square in the old town. You can also easily flag down a taxi along the north coast 'zone touristique'. If you want, you can hire a taxi by the day and do a grand tour of the island. You can also hire a **bicycle** or a **moped** from just about any hotel at a reasonable cost. It is possible to find **mountain bikes** (although there is a shortage of mountains).

Sfax
Mercure Sfax, Avenue Habib Bourguiba, tel: 74 225 700, fax: 74 225 521, www. mercure.com Mercure four-star comfort, just five minutes from the medina.
Borj Dhiafa, Km. 3, Soukra Road, Sfax, tel: 74 677 777, www.hotel-borjdhiafa.com Modern hotel built in the style of a traditional *borj* (fortified house), with 26 rooms, indoor pool, two restaurants and bar, furnished with handmade textiles and woodwork.

Kerkennah Islands
Seabel Grand Hotel, Zone Touristique, Sidi Fredj, tel: 74 489 877, www.grand-hotel-kerkennah.com.tn The biggest and best hotel on the island, with 94 rooms, all with private balcony. Though rated only two-star, it has good facilities, including an outdoor barbecue restaurant.

Gabès
Oasis Hotel, Beach Road, tel: 75 270 782/884, fax: 271 749. The top hotel on the beach.
Hotel Nejib, Avenue Farhat Hached, tel: 75 271 686/547, fax: 271 587. Best in town.
Chela Club, Beach Road, tel: 75 227 442, fax: 227 446. Large bungalow-style accommodation situated on the beach and surrounded by palms, but it can sometimes get crowded with groups.

Djerba
Radisson SAS Resort and Thalasso, tel: 75 757 600, www.radissonsas.com Newest five-star resort hotel on the island, with a strong claim to be the best in Djerba (and maybe in Tunisia). Excellent service and facilities.
Hasdrubal Thalassa Prestige/ Hasdrubal Thalassa and Spa, Beach Road, tel: 75 759 259 and 75 730 657, www.hasdrubal-thalassa.com and www.hasdrubal-hotel.com Twin five-star thalassotherapy hotels sharing resort facilities on the north coast.
Mövenpick Ulysse Palace and Thalasso, Beach Road, tel: 75 758 777, www.moevenpick.com Smart but friendly hotel with all the amenities.

Melia Palm Azur, Beach Road, tel: 75 750 700, www.sol melia.com High-class service and comfort in beach hotel.

Hotel Djerba Erriadh, 10 Avenue Mohamed Fergiani, tel: 75 650 756, e-mail: erriadh@ hotmail.com Former *fondouk* (merchants' inn) with 30 rooms and a pretty courtyard, in the heart of old Houmt Souk.

Dar Bibine, Erriadh, tel: 75 671 196, www.darbibine.com Gorgeous boutique hotel in the heart of a historic village in the centre of the island.

Dar Dhiafa, Erriadh, tel: 75 671 166, www.hoteldardhiafa.com Another addition to Djerba's growing portfolio of chic (and expensive) boutique hotels.

WHERE TO EAT

Sfax
Le Corail, 39 Rue Habib Maazoun, tel: 74 227 301, fax: 210 317. The smartest place in town serving fish specialities.

Le Printemps, 57 Avenue Bourguiba, tel: 74 226 973. A French restaurant in the mid-price range.

Bagdad, 63 Avenue Farhat Hached, tel: 74 223 085. More modest but still a good place at reasonable prices.

Gabès
el Mazar, 39 Avenue Farhat Hached, tel: 75 272 055. One of the smarter places in town. Expensive.

L'Oasis, 15 Avenue Farhat Hached, tel: 75 270 098. Near beach, good food; not cheap.

La Ruche, tel: 75 270 369. Moderate restaurant serving Tunisian cuisine.

Djerba
La Princesse D'Haroun, The Port, Houmt Souk, tel: 75 650 488/483, fax: 650 815. Lovely fish restaurant overlooking the port. The best on the island.

Restaurant Blue Moon, Place H Chaker, Houmt Souk, tel: 75 650 559. Traditional restaurant in the old town. Lovely open courtyard and local specialities.

El Farida, Casino de Djerba, Sidi Mahrez, tel: 75 757 537. Djerba's most expensive restaurant, with live entertainment from Tunisian musicians and a menu that emphasizes posh versions of traditional dishes.

TOURS AND EXCURSIONS

The Gulf of Gabès, and Djerba in particular, is ideally placed for **exploring the Ksour** (fortified Berber villages) of the south. Organized excursions may be booked from all main resort hotels and leave early to return late the same day. From Sfax, there are one-day tours available to the **Kerkennah Islands** and other places of interest. Alternatively,

you can go independently on the car ferry (*see* below).

USEFUL CONTACTS

Sfax Tourist Office, Chott El Kerekennah, tel/fax: 74 211 040.

Thyna Airport, tel: 74 278 000, fax: 279 411.

Train Station, Avenue Habib Bourguiba, tel: 74 221 999 (*ferroviaire*).

Car Ferry (to Kerkennah Islands), 5 Avenue Mohammed Hedi Kefacha, tel: 74 223 615.

Gabès Tourist Office, Avenue Hedi Chaker, tel: 75 270 254.

Train Station, Rue Mongi Slim, tel: 75 270 944 (*ferroviaire*).

Bus Station, Route de l'Oasis, tel: 75 272 300.

Djerba Tourist Office (Regional), Bvd de l'Environnement, Route de Sidi Mahrez, Houmt Souk, tel: 75 650 016, fax: 650 581.

Local Tourist Office, Place des Martyrs, Houmt Souk, tel: 75 650 915.

Midoun Tourist Office, tel: 75 657 114.

Police, tel: 75 650 015.

Hospital, Avenue Habib Bourguiba, Houmt Souk, tel: 75 650 018.

GABES	J	F	M	A	M	J	J	A	S	O	N	D
AVERAGE TEMP. °F	61	64	69	74	79	83	89	91	87	81	72	63
AVERAGE TEMP. °C	16	18	21	23	26	28	32	33	31	27	22	17
RAINFALL in	0.9	0.7	0.8	0.4	0.3	0	0	0.1	0.5	1.2	1.2	0.6
RAINFALL mm	23	18	20	10	8	0	0	3	13	31	31	15
DAYS OF RAINFALL	4	3	4	3	2	0	0	1	3	4	4	4

7
The South and the Desert

As the beaches and cities of the coast give way to the Sahara, Tunisia reveals a different face, one that is seemingly endless and remote, its sand seas and desert mountains punctuated by **Berber villages** and cool **oases**. Most desert people still live a traditional life, although tourists have made some impact on their economy and way of life. The idea of getting away from the resorts on the coast seems to becoming more and more popular and, as a result, the quality of hotels in the desert areas has become more enticing – some being very luxurious indeed. Other visitors, however, prefer the simplicity of a safari across the sands and a tent under the stars.

CHOTT EL JERID

The country is almost halved by the Chott El Jerid, an expansive **salt-pan** fringed by the large **oasis towns** of Tozeur, Nefta and Kebili, as well as smaller oases. Until the tarmac causeway was completed in 1984, you had to drive across the vast expanse of salt crust to reach the western oases of Tozeur, Douz and Nefta. The firm surface is often thin and conceals a soft, muddy underside. In the old days, there were often tales of travellers sinking without trace into the ooze; one such tale recounts the loss of a thousand camels from a caravan.

Today, however, the *chott* is a centre for **sand yachting**: the crisp, crystalline surface ideal for high-speed racing. For the less adventurous, simply drive across on the road and watch the action. During the summer, flocks of flamingos and other **water birds** wade through the shallows.

DON'T MISS

** **The palmery at Nefta:** swaying palms and bathing pools.
** **The Roman pools at Gafsa:** unmatched atmosphere and history.
*** **The Red Lizard Train:** a sensational ride through the desert gorges.
*** **Chebika:** the perfect example of a mountain oasis.
*** **Matmata:** underground houses and hotels.
*** **Chenini:** spectacular location and an authentic Berber village.

Opposite: *The stark beauty of the desert near Tataouine attracts explorers and dreamers alike.*

THE SOUTH AND THE DESERT CLIMATE

The south of Tunisia is extremely hot and arid. All water is underground in aquifers and agriculture is generally only possible in the **oases** where water is pumped up from springs.

Travel in the **summer** can be staggeringly hot and uncomfortable; even in **winter** the Saharan regions can be hot – although the temperature can plunge to freezing at night.

The extent of the *chott* is enormous – almost 250km (150 miles) by 20km (13 miles) – and it is the largest in the entire Sahara desert. Fantastic plans to run a canal across the *chott* in the late 19th century came to nothing, as did the even more bizarre plan to blast a lake-sized hole in the *chott* with a nuclear bomb.

Small communities surrounding the *chott* depend on underground water for their existence and in some places **springs** gush out into hot pools, such as those at Tozeur.

GAFSA

Gafsa is the regional capital and lies to the north of the Chott El Jerid. Known in Roman times as **Capsa**, the site was originally settled during the Stone Age – lending its name to the early human 'Capsian Man'. The strategic position of the town accounts for its apparently continuous occupation over the centuries.

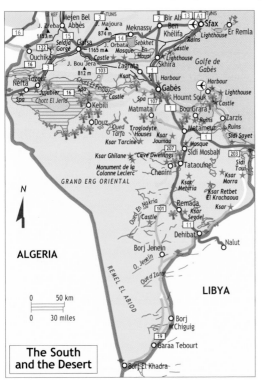

The South and the Desert

Early Gafsa

During Carthaginian rule, Gafsa featured a **Berber fortress**, but during the Roman era the town was added to the long list of Saharan settlements which joined the Roman Empire. Roman Capsa became a rich trading town under the emperor **Trajan** and an important asset to the Romans. It remained so throughout the Byzantine era, and when the Arab armies took the town in 668AD, it remained Romanized for some centuries afterward.

Gafsa's Kasbah *

The kasbah was built by the **Hafsites** in 1434 but was captured in 1556 by **Dragut** who had allied with the Ottomans. Unfortunately, however, this centuries-old edifice was badly damaged when an arsenal exploded nearby in World War II.

Other places of interest are the two **Roman pools**, the larger of which is in a picturesque setting, flanked by the arches of the Bey's palace and swaying palm trees. Young boys dive into the water, sometimes from a great height, and expect tourists to tip them for their efforts.

Above: *A ride on the 19th-century Red Lizard train is a must for all railway buffs.*

Gafsa's Great Mosque *

The Great Mosque is also well worth seeing. Restored in 1969, it has a tall, square **minaret** which offers a panoramic view of the town.

The Red Lizard Train ***

This grand folly of a train was built to order by the Bey of Tunis in the late 19th century. The circular line which takes the train up through the dramatic **Seldja Gorge** starts and finishes at Metlaoui station. The train is pulled by a diesel locomotive and has five carriages, all restored now to something of their former glory. Train buffs will be delighted with authentic wood panelling and red velvet upholstery, and even the light fittings are authentic. True to its name, the outside of the carriages are painted in red livery. The circuit takes about 1½ hours and runs Sun–Fri, leaving at 11:00. There are no trains on Saturdays. For more information, contact Transtours, tel: 76 240 634. The train's terminus, Metlaoui, is a rather ugly industrial settlement involved in the phosphate mining business. Despite the unpromising start, the scenery on the ride is both dramatic and beautiful.

CAMEL WRESTLING

The sport of camel wrestling occurs throughout the Middle East and North Africa, although it is not very common these days. The best opportunities to catch sight of this ancient contest of strength are at the **festivals** held in the desert regions of Tunisia during winter.

The 'action' in the wrestling contests is often over very quickly, with a decisive victory going to the strongest, if not the boldest, male camel. Young males of about two years old are used in the sport and they basically use their immense necks to overthrow their opponent. Although the camels make a loud moaning noise during the contest, neither animal is hurt by the wrestling.

Right: *The old medina in Tozeur is built with mud bricks in a distinctive geometric design.*

THE MOUNTAIN OASES

As you draw closer to the Algerian border in the west, the landscape becomes more mountainous. In the hills are a number of mountain oases.

Chebika **

The most visited of the mountain oases is Chebika, a text-book example of an oasis with its **palm trees**, **olives** and smaller shrubs, such as **pomegranate**, planted between. The village high on the bluff is now in ruins but the oasis below is alive and fed by irrigation canals. Water cascades down crevasses in the limestone rocks into pools below. Locals crack open rocks to reveal crystal formations which you can buy for a few dinars.

Tamerza **

Further to the north, close to the Algerian border and perched on either side of a wadi, is Tamerza, an old desert village abandoned following a freak flood many years ago. The surviving buildings show the traditional Saharan architecture of the region. Behind the derelict village is a large **palmery** which is still active and productive. Across the wadi is the new town, which boasts a recently built four-star hotel that is so well designed it virtually disappears into the hillside. You can swim in the pool and gaze out across the wadi.

TOZEUR

The old **medina** in this oasis town is built with mud bricks laid out in striking geometric patterns, a style which is only found elsewhere in neighbouring Nefta. The town's Roman origins are concealed beneath several layers of buildings and all that remains are eroded capitals and giant oil jars in the **Traditional and Archaeological Museum**. Tusuros – as it was called – was an outpost on the desert trading route, popular no doubt for its 200 springs which feed the oasis.

The main attraction is the **palmery**, which covers 10km² (4 sq miles) and has over 250,000 trees. Take a tour of the oasis by horse or camel or by horse-drawn calash.

The town's privately owned **Dar Cheraït Museum** is open daily 08:00–24:00. It is a converted old house displaying historical tableaux from Tunisian life, and includes a good collection of antique furniture.

CAMPING IN THE DESERT

If you intend spending a night under the Saharan sky, be aware of some safety rules:
● Make sure someone knows where you are going and when you expect to arrive. Inform the **National Guard** at the check-points or the local **police**.
● Check your **vehicle** for roadworthiness and be sure to have spares and tools.
● Take plenty of **water** to cover delays or mishaps (5 litres/9 pints per person).
● If you break down in the desert **don't**, whatever you do, leave your vehicle and wander off to find help.

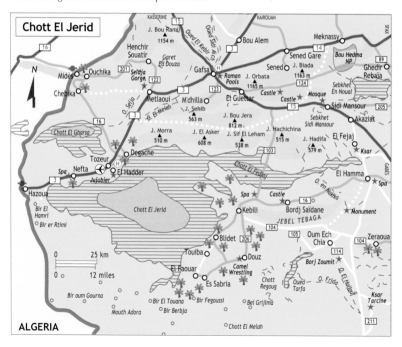

Nefta **

The attractive oasis of Nefta is one of the most important religious centres in Tunisia, steeped in the **Sufi tradition** – a mystical branch of Islam. As a result, the old part of town is crammed with shrines and mosques which sit almost side by side along the twisting, narrow streets.

The town's main industry is **weaving** and streets are also lined with shops hung with colourful **kelims** and **wall-hangings** in geometric designs that reflect those on the mud-brick buildings of the area.

The palmery at Nefta is in a *corbeille*, a crater-like depression, with a series of open pools at the bottom. These are used for bathing and often have an unofficial rota for the different sexes. There is also a **hot spring** in the town.

Above: *In Douz the spice market is full of delicious aromas and exotic colours.*

STAR WARS

When they were looking for alien planet locations for the blockbuster *Star Wars*, the film makers chose **Matmata**. A **troglodyte house** was Luke Skywalker's home and the famous bar scene was shot in the lobby of the **Hotel Sidi Driss**. It is not surprising that Matmata was chosen as the location – the resemblance to a fantasy moonscape is remarkable. Many movie buffs make the pilgrimage to see the locations and stay in the 'Star Wars' hotel.

DOUZ

Douz is a town with few natural attractions, but once a year – in winter sometime – it comes alive for the week-long **Douz festival**, in which all manner of traditional events take place. Started in the mid-1970s as a way of keeping local folklore and tradition alive, it soon began attracting large numbers of foreign visitors, some of whom come to Tunisia especially for the festival. Apart from the expert horsemanship, there are various races with camels and the rare opportunity to see **camel wrestling** (*see* panel, page 113). The festival is a lively and colourful display with men and women in local costumes from all over the south.

For the rest of the year, Douz thrives on organizing **desert safaris** and quite rightly calls itself 'Gateway of the Desert'. From here to the south is the Sahara of the imagination; sand dunes, palm oases and dramatic skies. Be warned, though, the temperatures in summer can be dangerously high. The regular lively **market** on

Thursdays attracts people from far and wide and you can make all sorts of purchases here: sand roses from the desert, robes and sandals, and dates, of course. Most visitors, however, soon head for the livestock section to see the **camels**.

MATMATA

Matmata is named after the tribe who inhabit the region, but these days the town is best known for its **underground houses**. As in Bulla Regia, the Berbers of Matmata excavated their houses from the sandstone to escape the intense heat of summer. The tradition dates back at least 400 years. Although there is a new town below, many people still inhabit the old settlement. In fact, some of the houses have been turned into **troglodyte hotels**, and other households make a living selling souvenirs.

Needless to say, Matmata is a tourist honeypot with many coach trips stopping for a visit. The result is not to everyone's taste: some of the locals find the intrusion too much. Even so, Matmata is a fascinating place, especially in low season and if you stay overnight.

THE KSOUR

The extreme southern region of Tunisia, south of Djerba, is the most unspoilt part of the country. It has a string of **Berber villages** stretching down the hillside into the desert towards the border with Libya.

Historically, the region was famous for both its fierce independence of authority and its **banditry** – should anyone be foolish enough to travel unprotected – and even the African explorers of the 19th century gave the area a wide berth.

THE DOUZ FESTIVAL

The festival, with its many **parades** of tribespeople in extraordinary **costumes**, is held over three days in the desert outside the town. Men and women both take part and you can see a traditional camel-back **wedding** procession, complete with *howdah*, housing the bride perched on the camel's back. Other events include **camel wrestling** and **hare coursing**.

Below: *Camel riders gather to race at the Douz Festival, held every winter.*

Below: *The restored ksar at Medenine is often used for displays of traditional music and dancing.*

The term 'Ksour' is the plural of ksar, meaning a fortified **granary**, and these wonderful constructions are a feature right across the high escarpment which ends at Garyan in Libya. Built of mud brick, they are composed of dozens of honeycomb-like **cells**, called *ghorfas*, in which grain and oil were stored. Each family would have a cell, and deposits and withdrawals were logged by a keeper – much like a modern bank. In times of attack, their impenetrable outer walls made them a safe haven for people.

Medenine ★★

Medenine is the main market town of the area and the usual starting point for a trip around the Ksour. Medenine's own large ksar has been mostly destroyed but the courtyard is still visible. Although the *ghorfas* here have been turned into shops, just behind these are some abandoned *ghorfas* which give a clearer idea of their original appearance. If you have little time for exploring the region, head 6km (3½ miles) west to the village of **Metameur** to see the ksar at the high point of the village.

The main route south to Tataouine is dull so it is better to take a detour through Ksar Joumaa and Beni Khaddache across the mighty **Jebel Dahar** – some of the most dramatic scenery in all Tunisia. At **Ksar Joumaa** is a striking hill-top ksar which appears rather plain from the outside but is fascinating inside.

Tataouine **

Around Tataouine you will find some of the most beautiful **scenery** in all of Tunisia. The area is sprinkled with Berber villages and numerous **springs** (the word *tataouine* literally means 'the mouth of the springs'). The ksar here is just a few kilometres out of town on the Remada road, and it takes approximately an hour to walk up to it – to be met with truly spectacular **views** of the town and surroundings.

Above: *A simple farmhouse nestles beneath the mountains of the Ksour.*

Chenini **

Nearby Chenini is not to be missed. Approximately 18km (11 miles) to the west of Tataouine, it is perched in a magnificent setting high up on an escarpment. The entire village is a well-preserved working example of a Berber mountain village and, in fact, the ksar is still in use, keeping the grain in perfect condition for up to 10 years. Close by are the shrine and graves of the mysterious '**seven sleepers**': the grave mounds are 5m (16½ft) long and there are in fact 11 of them in the area. Naturally the graves are subject to many rather intriguing local legends.

Beyond Chenini

Further to the south is **Douiret**, another picturesque village high on the mountain which is in a reasonably good state of preservation. Even more remote is **Ksar Ouled Soltane**, which has the best preserved ksar in the south, with four-storey *ghorfas*. It is one of the last villages you will encounter before you reach the Libyan border. There is nothing to do in these villages apart from wander around on foot, but they offer a really fascinating insight into Berber life.

> **TROGLODYTE HOUSES**
>
> Where the rock is of workable sandstone interleaved with harder layers of limestone, the **Berbers** chose to carve their houses out of the living rock. There are two basic kinds of Berber troglodyte dwelling: pit style or hillside type. The first is excavated vertically into a round or square **pit** and then rooms are hewn out horizontally. For access a sloping **tunnel** is made with side rooms for animals. There are usually bedrooms and storage rooms on all sides of the courtyard. In the centre is usually a well.
>
> In the hillside dwellings, the houses are often stacked on top of one another – or hewn out side by side – on the slopes. They each have a private **courtyard** surrounded by a wall for privacy.

The South and the Desert at a Glance

BEST TIMES TO VISIT

The heat of summer can make travelling in the south of Tunisia very uncomfortable. Also, apart from in the main towns, there are few luxuries such as swimming pools and air conditioning to make life easier. Best times to go are **spring** and **autumn**, though it will still be hot. However, one of the most popular times to visit Tunisia is in the **winter** when the Douz and Sahara Festivals take place. The timing of these two festivals means that you can attend both. If you plan to stay in Douz be sure to book well in advance – it's well worth it.

GETTING THERE

There are five flights a week between Tozeur and Tunis, and one flight per week between Tozeur and Djerba, all on Tunis Air. There are also direct international flights from several European cities to Tozeur. From there, you can connect to the other desert towns – Nefta, Gabès, Gafsa and Douz – by **bus**. The only mountain oasis with a bus service is Tamerza which connects to Gafsa. To visit Matmata, take a bus from Gabès (or else take the daily bus from Tunis, which takes approximately 5½ hours). In addition to the buses, *louages* run between all the main towns and some of the smaller ones.

GETTING AROUND

The south of Tunisia is not great for public transport but it is still possible to tour this region using the **buses** and *louages*. A little planning will save you getting stuck in an out-of-the-way place. If there are several of you travelling in a group, consider hiring a **taxi** by the day for tailor-made sightseeing. The cost should be negotiated beforehand but can work out to be quite inexpensive.

WHERE TO STAY

When it comes to hotel accommodation, there is not a great deal of choice in many desert towns; your best bet is to go to Tozeur and Nefta, which have a selection of reasonably comfortable hotels. In the more remote places, there may be only one hotel – or none at all – so it is important to check before setting out. For something different, try the troglodyte hotels in Matmata.

Tozeur
Dar Cheraît, Route Touristique, 2200 Tozeur, tel: 76 454 888/880, 453 311, fax: 453 271, www.darcherait.com.tn
This is the best hotel in town. Five stars and it shows – good food, good service.
Sofitel Tozeur Palm Beach, Route Touristique, 2200 Tozeur, tel: 76 453 111/ 211/311, fax: 453 911/454/

288, www.sofitel.com
One of the better tourist hotels in town.
Grand Hotel de l'Oasis, Place des Martyres, tel: 76 452 300, fax: 452 153. Another of Tozeur's new ultra-smart hotels.
Residence Warda, Avenue Abou Al Kacem Chabbi, tel: 76 452 597, fax: 452 744. This is a good value-for-money budget hotel which is family-run and spotlessly clean. It is situated right on the edge of the palmery.

Gafsa
Hotel Maamoun, Route de Gabès, tel: 76 220 470, 224 441, 222 740/433, fax: 226 440. Popular with tour groups, this hotel is quite comfortable but rather expensive for what it offers.
The Gafsa Hotel, Rue Ahmed Senoussi, tel: 76 224 000, 225 000, 223 000, fax: 224 747. A Mid-range hotel which is plain but comfortable. It has heating in the winter, which is important at night.

Nefta
Bel Horizon, Cite Corbeille, Avenue 7 Novembre, 2240 Nefta, tel: 76 430 088, fax: 430 500.

Douz
Melia El-Mouradi Oasis, Zone Touristique, BP 155, 4260 Douz, tel: 75 470 303, fax: 470 905/906, www.elmouradi.com

The South and the Desert at a Glance

Tamerza

Tamerza Palace, Zone Touristique, 2200 Tamerza, tel: 76 485 322/344/345, fax: 453 722, www.tamerza-palace.com The best desert hotel in Tunisia, with a terrace pool overlooking the wadi. Wonderful food and organic architecture.

Hotel des Cascades, the Palmery, tel: 76 453 732. Right in the heart of the oasis. It has a pool and showers. The restaurant is average.

Matmata

Ksar Amazigh, Route de Tamezret, 6070, Matmata, tel: 75 230 088/062, fax: 230 273. One of a handful of troglodyte hotels in Matmata.

Hotel Sidi Driss, tel: 75 230 005. Famous as the location of the bar scene in *Star Wars*. Long on character, short on luxury, but who cares in this wonderful place?

Matmata Hotel, BP 64, 6070 Matmata, tel: 75 230 066, fax: 230 177. This is not a troglodyte hotel but it does have a swimming pool.

Tataouine

Dakyanus, BP 234, Zone Al-Ferch, 3200 Tataouine, tel: 75 832 199, fax: 832 198.

Most **hotels** serve a combination of European cuisine and traditional Tunisian cooking, of reasonable quality. Outside the main desert towns, eating

out is a rather limited experience. You can always find a **small restaurant** serving simple, tasty dishes, though, and it's a good way to sample the local specialities. If you want something more memorable, the restaurant at the **Tamerza Hotel** is great but rather expensive. In **Tozeur**, try the **Petit Prince**, overlooking the palmery and, in **Nefta**, there is a **bar/restaurant** in the **palmery** which serves simple grills and cold beer.

You can either make a trip to the **desert** as part of a beach-based holiday or head for the desert for the main event. If you just want a break from sunbathing there are various itineraries leaving from Djerba or the other coastal resorts which give a taste of the Sahara. Allow three days to do this properly, with two nights sleeping out.

Douz Voyages, Place de l'Independence, Douz, tel: 75 470 178/179, fax: 470 315; Route de l'Aeroport, Djerba, tel: 75 652 778, fax: 653 514, www.chez.com/douz

voyages/ One of the best agencies for desert trips, with long experience of desert expeditions.

Carthage Tours, Avenue Farhat Hached, Tozeur, tel: 76 451 300, fax: 452 409/377, www.carthage-tours.com

Passion de Voyages, Tozeur, tel: 76 451 039/034.

Tamerza Palace Hotel (reservations for the Red Lizard Train), tel: 76 485 322, fax: 453 722, www.tamerza-palace.com

Gafsa Tourist Office, Place des Piscines Romaines, tel: 76 221 664.

Gafsa Train Station (*gare ferroviaire*), tel: 76 270 482.

Gafsa Bus Station (*gare routiere*), tel: 76 221 587.

Regional Tourist Office, Avenue Aboulkacem Chebbi, Tozeur, tel: 76 454 503, fax: 452 051.

Nefta Tourist Office, Avenue Habib Bourguiba, tel: 76 430 236.

Douz Tourist Office, Place des Martyrs, tel: 75 470 351.

Tataouine Police, Place des Martyrs, tel: 76 860 814.

GAFSA	J	F	M	A	M	J	J	A	S	O	N	D
AVERAGE TEMP. °F	58	62	69	77	85	94	101	100	92	81	69	59
AVERAGE TEMP. °C	14	17	21	25	29	34	38	38	33	27	21	15
RAINFALL in	0.7	0.5	0.9	0.6	0.4	0.3	0.1	0.2	0.5	0.5	0.7	0.5
RAINFALL mm	18	13	23	15	10	8	3	5	13	13	18	13
DAYS OF RAINFALL	3	3	3	3	3	1	1	1	3	3	3	3

Travel Tips

Tourist Information

There are **National Tourist Board** offices in most European capitals including London, Paris, Brussels, Stockholm, Rome, Frankfurt, Vienna, Madrid and Amsterdam. The head office in Tunis is at 1 Avenue Mohammed V, tel: 71 341 077, and there are regional **Tourist Offices** (ONTT) in all the main tourism centres in Tunisia – all with a good selection of brochures and area maps. Smaller places have local **Syndicats d'Inititative** offices which hand out local information and are identified by a blue-and-red sign.

Entry Requirements

Citizens of all EU countries, most other European countries, the USA and Canada may enter Tunisia without a visa and may stay for up to three months. Citizens of most other countries may buy a visa on arrival, but rules may change: check the requirements for your nationality before departure. Airlines may refuse to carry you if your passport and visa are not in order.

Customs

Currently, you can bring in the following **duty free** allowances: one litre of spirits, two litres of wine, 200 cigarettes or 50 cigars or 400g (14 ounces) tobacco. Other goods to the value of £140 Sterling (check specifics with Tourist Board). If you have more than the allowance (a camera kit with several cameras etc.), customs officers will write details in your passport. **Important:** be sure to get the equipment checked out when you leave the country. The import or export of Tunisian currency is forbidden. You may bring in any amount of foreign currency and re-export it but you must declare any amount in excess of the equivalent of TD500 on arrival. When leaving the country you may only reconvert up to 30% of the dinars you exchanged on your visit and you must show all your currency exchange receipts as proof.

Health Requirements

There are no compulsory inoculations required for Tunisia.

Getting There

By Air: There are scheduled flights from many European and Middle Eastern capitals to Tunis; the best connections for travellers from outside Europe are via Paris, London and Rome. Cheaper charter flights operate from the UK mainly to Monastir; try **Thomas Cook Airlines** (www.thomascook airlines.co.uk) for flights from many UK airports. The largest airport on the African continent is set to open at Enfidha (midway between Monastir and Tunis) in 2009/2010 and is expected to open up Tunisia to many more low-cost flights.

By Sea: Tunisian company **CTN** (www.ctn.com.tn) and French ferry line **SNCM** (www.sncm.fr) sail weekly in winter and several times weekly in summer from Marseille and Genoa to Tunis. Italian line **Grandi Navi Veloci** (www.gnv.it) also sails from Genoa.

What to Pack

Summer in Tunisia can be extremely hot so it is best to pack lightweight, casual clothing that can be easily laundered. For protection against the harsh sun, a good pair of sunglasses and a straw hat are also recommended. Away from the tourist resorts, you'll need to cover up a little more so lightweight cotton trousers and a sleeved top are advisable. Women who plan to visit a mosque should remember to take a headscarf.

If you are planning to visit the Sahara, remember that the sun can be very intense indeed. In addition to the above, it is a good idea to take a cotton scarf to cover your neck which is very prone to bad sunburn. Needless to say, a good quality suncream is a must.

Depending on where you are staying, it is advisable to take something smart but casual for the evening. Resorts tend to be informal but, in the city, something smarter might be in order. A sweater or jacket is useful in the evenings when the temperature drops, especially in the desert. Tunisia can be quite wet in winter, so take a light waterproof to wear over your sweater.

Money Matters

Currency: Tunisia's unit of currency is the dinar, divided into 1000 millimes. Notes come in denominations of 5, 10, 20 and 30TD. There are also ½-, 1- and 5-dinar coins.

Exchange: Airport bureaux de change are open from 07:00 until the last plane arrives. Regular banks are open different hours during the season; 1 October–1 July, they are open Mon–Fri, 08:00–11:00 and 14:00–16:00; for the rest of the year, they are open 07:30–11:00 or 08:00–12:00. Hours are reduced during the holy month of Ramadan, the dates of which change each year. You can also change money at most hotels and some travel agencies.

Credit cards: Major credit cards are accepted at larger hotels, car-rental agencies and some restaurants and smarter shops, but souks and small shops usually only accept cash. For all credit card and exchange transactions, you will need to have your passport with you.

Tipping: Gratuities are not obligatory but are usually expected. It is usually sufficient to round off a bill with a small extra sum. For porters and lavatory attendants, 200 millimes is enough per bag or per visit. Waiters should be tipped 10–15%, as should tour guides.

Accommodation

The Tunisian government has a hotel rating system between one and five stars which also governs the prices they may charge. Most accommodation falls into the tourist class of 3 or 4 stars and these **hotels** are clean and comfortable, often with sports facilities and swimming pools. Below this level, you can often find lovely traditional hotels which are also clean but without the fancy trappings of the larger places. Most towns also have a collection of much cheaper, unclassified hotels – often in the old medinas – and these can be more than adequate and a lot more interesting than package tourist hotels.

Camping is a recent development and several sites have opened at various places including Hamman-Lif, Hammamet, Gabès, Nabeul, Tozeur and Zarzis. The cost for camping should not be more than 2TD per person per night. Unofficial camping is tolerated in the northern beach areas.

Eating Out

There is no shortage of choices for eating out in Tunisia. From a simple couscous to a four-course meal, eating out can be a rewarding experience whatever your budget. **Tourist hotels** tend to cater for international tastes with only a nod towards traditional food, but **restaurants** in the towns and villages serve all kinds of food. In the larger places, you will also find French- and Italian-style restaurants as well as pizzas and **fast food**. A full meal with wine in a good restaurant should cost no more than 35TD (per person), very

GOOD READING

Knapp, W. *Tunisia* (Thames & Hudson, 1970).

Broughton, Broderick. *Parts of Barbary* (Hutchinson, 1943).

Carrington, R. *East From Tunis* (Chatto & Windus, 1957).

Furlonge, G. *The Lands of Barbary* (John Murray, 1966).

Petrie, G. *Tunis, Kairouan & Carthage* (reprinted by Darf, 1985).

Valenski, L. & Udovitch, A. *The Last Arab Jews* (Harwood Academic Publishers, 1985).

Flaubert, Gustave. *Salammbô* (Penguin, 1987).

Ondaatje, M. *The English Patient* (Random House, 1992).

much less in a smaller establishment. Not all restaurants serve alcohol – only those in more sophisticated parts of Tunis, tourist resorts (and not always even there). If a glass of wine or beer is a priority, check before you take a seat.

Transport

Train: There is a good, efficient and cheap railway network with air-conditioned trains run by SNCFT on the main routes. The main routes run from Tunis, north to Bizerte, west to Guardimao, southwest to Kalaa Kasbah and south to Cap Bon, Gabès and Gafsa. There are connections onward to Hammamet, Nabeul and Sousse, with a few trains going on to Sfax and El Jem. One train a day goes from Sfax to Gafsa and Metlaoui where you pick up the circular Red Lizard Train through the Seldja Gorge.

Road: Car rental in Tunisia is very expensive and not really necessary unless you want to visit some out-of-the-way ruins or small villages in the south that are poorly served by buses. You will need a valid license at least one year old. If you are bringing your own vehicle, then you will also need your car registration document (or *Carte grise*) and proof of insurance (although you can buy third-party insurance at the port of entry or the land border). Driving is on the right with a maximum speed limit of 90kph (56mph) on the open road and 50kph (30mph) in built up areas. Petrol prices are not that cheap – about the same as the UK – and petrol stations can be infrequent off the main highways. There are frequent check-points along the road and it is a good idea to have all your car papers and passport to hand at all times.

Bus: Travelling by bus is cheap and the routes are comprehensive and convenient. Most of the main services are run by the Société Nationale de Transport which tie in with local services run by Société Regionale de Transport (although, to confuse things, the latter also run inter-city services). Tunis, Bizerte and Sfax have separate bus stations for these two companies but, in smaller towns, there is just the one. It is worth remembering that they have separate time-tables, so be sure to check both for the earliest departure. Tickets must be bought from the relevant ticket office before departure.

Louage/Taxi: Shared taxis, known as *louages*, are the means of transport used by the locals. These are yellow Peugeot cars of various vintages converted to carry the maximum number of people at high speed around the country. They operate on a 'wait until full' basis and are cheap, if not exactly a luxurious means of transport. Faster than buses, they congregate at one or more points in town and usually shout their destination. If you are going to an unpopular place, there may be a bit of a wait while the car fills up.

Regular taxis come in two varieties, *petit* taxis and *grand* taxis. The former takes up to three passengers and the latter five. These are metered and amazingly cheap, but a warning – taxi touts at airports are not metered and are out to overcharge you. *Don't use these.* Private taxis can be hired for a day, but be sure to negotiate the price beforehand.

Air: There are several internal air routes served by Tunis Air (www.tunisair.com) and Tunisavia (www.tunisavia.com.tn) The destinations are: Djerba, Monastir, Tozeur, Gabès and Sfax. The Tunis–Djerba route is very popular and often fully booked, so plan ahead if you want to use this route. Booking numbers in Tunis are: Tunis Air (airport) tel: 71 754 000 or 755 000; Tunisavia, tel: 71 717 600. Flights are frequent (there are about six per day to Djerba) and not more than one hour long.

Business Hours

Tunisia operates on a Monday to Friday working week with Saturday and Sunday off for all government departments and most offices. The exception is the tourist business, where offices such as car-hire companies and tour operators open long hours and weekends to accommodate holidaymakers.

Time Difference

Time in Tunisia is on Central European Time, one hour ahead of Greenwich Mean Time. There is no daylight saving scheme.

Communications

Tunisia's **telephone** system is now mostly direct dial. There are callboxes, **Taxiphones**, where you can make local calls. They take 50-millime coins and are found in stations, airports cafés and public places. For long distance, you have to call either through a **hotel switchboard** or use the post office **telephone bureau**. In Tunis, the telephone bureau in the main post office is open 24 hours.

Post offices are signposted with a yellow sign with black Arabic lettering. There is a small PTT sign in the corner of it. Opening hours vary according to time of year: 16 September to 30 June, 08:00–12:00 and 15:00–18:00 Mon–Fri, and 08:00–12:00 Saturday; 1 July to 15 September, 07:30–12:30 and 16:30–18:30 Mon–Fri. During Ramadan, hours are 09:00–13:30 Mon–Sat. If you don't know where you will be staying and want to receive letters, use the **Poste Restante** service. Have your letters addressed 'Poste Restante' and the name of the town. When you collect your mail, there is a small charge and you will need your passport.

Internet access is patchy and slow, even in large business hotels, some of which have wireless connectivity in public areas. **Publinet** Internet centres can be found in most towns and resorts. Anglophone touch-typists may find these frustrating, as they all have French-style AZERTY and Arabic keyboards instead of the familiar QWERTY keys.

Mobile phone coverage is good (but very expensive) over most of the country but patchy in the deep desert areas. Beware using **hotel phones** which are universally extortionately over-priced.

Electricity

220-volt, 50-cycle AC is now standard throughout Tunisia, except perhaps in some of the older parts of Tunis. The current is still prone to surges so beware when using a computer and unplug all appliances when not in use. British 240-volt appliances will run quite well on 220 volts with an adapter.

Weights and Measures

Tunisia uses the metric system for all measurements.

Health Precautions

Although no compulsory inoculations are required for Tunisia, for added security it is a good idea to have up-to-date **tetanus**, **polio**, **cholera** and **typhoid** jabs. There is a small risk of **hepatitis** in the south of the country.

To avoid **diarrhoea**, drink only bottled water and eat only peeled fruit – and be careful of raw salads if you are in doubt about the hygiene of the restaurant. For those prone to runny tummy, carry immodium as an emergency measure.

Health Services

There is an abundance of **pharmacies** in Tunisia, always

CONVERSION CHART		
FROM	**TO**	**MULTIPLY BY**
Millimetres	Inches	0.0394
Centimetres	Inches	0.3937
Metres	Yards	1.0936
Metres	Feet	3.281
Kilometres	Miles	0.6214
Square kilometres	Square miles	0.386
Hectares	Acres	2.471
Litres	Pints	1.760
Kilograms	Pounds	2.205
Tonnes	Tons	0.984
To convert Celsius to Fahrenheit: x 9 ÷ 5 + 32		

run by knowledgeable pharmacists who will help you with your complaint. They can prescribe drugs for most common complaints without you having to see a **doctor**. If your problems are more serious, the pharmacist will recommend a local doctor.

Security

All the larger hotels have their own **security staff**, mainly to ensure that non-residents are kept out and thus reduce the risk of having your room burgled. Wherever large groups of foreign tourists congregate, minor thefts are inevitable, though in Tunisia the number is relatively small. Take sensible precautions and you should be perfectly safe. As most thefts occur in hotel rooms it really is worthwhile to lock up any valuables in the **hotel safe**, or carry them with you at all times. If you are staying in a small hotel ask the manager to lock your valuable things in his office. Once made responsible he will make sure they are safe.

Emergencies

The number throughout Tunisia for all the **emergency**

USEFUL PHRASES

English = *Arabic*
Hello (informal) • *Marhaba*
Hello (formal) • *As-Salam Alaykum*
Hello (reply) • *Wa'alaykum as-Salaam*
Goodbye • *Ma'a Salaama*
Yes • *Ayywa*
No • *La*
Please • *'afak/'afik/'afakum (m/f/pl)*
Thank you • *shukran*
I don't understand • *ma fhemtesh*
How much? • *bi kam?*
Too much • *ghalee*

---

services is: 197. In Tunis you can also call: **Fire** 198, **Ambulance** 190.
The special **snake-bite clinic** in Tunis is at Institute Pasteur, Place du Gouvernment.

Etiquette

Tunisians are tolerant people when it comes to foreign tourists. However, it is worth remembering that, once away from the hotel and beach complexes, Tunisia is a Muslim country and **dress** and **behaviour** should be appropriate. For men and women alike, it is bad manners to wander around in shorts (although this is often ignored). Women should cover up their arms and legs and, if visiting a **mosque**, should also wrap a headscarf around their head and shoulders.
If invited into a **Tunisian home**, it is polite to remove your shoes at the door. You will probably be offered tea or coffee and it is rude to refuse at least one cup.

ROAD SIGNS

Road signs are bilingual in French and Arabic. Most signs follow the French system. 'Toutes directions' will lead you through a town and 'Autres directions' will steer you around it. 'Zone Touristique' indicates the hotel district for tourists.

Language

Arabic is the mother tongue of Tunisians but **French** is also widely spoken – especially in the cities and tourist resorts.
In most of the larger hotels, **English** is spoken up to a point, as well as some **German** or **Italian**, depending on the clientele. In **Berber villages**, the local language may be the only one understood, with a smattering of Arabic thrown in.

NUMBERS

0 • sifr
1 • wahad
2 • itnayn
3 • talaata
4 • arbah
5 • khamsa
6 • sitta
7 • sabah
8 • tamanya
9 • tesah
10 • ashara
11 • hidashar
12 • itnashar
13 • talatashar
14 • arbatashar
15 • khamastashar
16 • sittashar
17 • sabahtashar
19 • tisatashar
20 • ishrin
21 • wahd wi'ishrin
30 • talatin
40 • arba'in
50 • khamsin
60 • sittin
70 • sab'in
80 • tamanin
90 • tis'in
100 • miyya
500 • khamasa miyya
1000 • alf

INDEX

Note: Numbers in **bold** indicate photographs